THE PILOT FACTOR

A fresh introduction to CRM

Jean Denis Marcellin

Available from Amazon.com and other retail outlets
Available on Kindle and other devices

http://www.planesimplesolutions.com

Table of Content

Dedication

This book is dedicated to my two aviation mentors and "parents".
To Alan, for taking me under your wing as your own, and instilling in me the love for perfection. Thank you for always believing and supporting me since the day we met.
To Sue, for adopting me as one of your aviation "sons", and teaching me that integrity matters before all. Thank you for the countless hours of conversation, and for always being there in time of need.
I also bear a grateful heart for the unconditional support and help of my two aviation heroes, Karlene & Eric.

"*I have come to accept the feeling of not knowing where I am going. And I have trained myself to love it. Because it is only when we are suspended in mid-air with no landing in sight, that we force our wings to unravel and alas begin our flight. And as we fly, we still may not know where we are going to. But the miracle is in the unfolding of the wings. You may not know where you're going, but you know that so long as you spread your wings, the winds will carry you.*"

— C. JOYBELL C.

When I stumbled onto Jean Denis Marcellin's blog, I was so impressed that I wrote an extra post for my own blog entitled, "My Favorite Bloggers"—with JD as the headliner!

JD specializes in the Human Factor side of flying. We pilots tend to be Type A problem solvers ("Eagles," according to his insightful analyses), and have an innate disdain for all that "charm school stuff." Emotional sensitivity is for sissies—I'm Captain Kirk, dammit!

Well, JD is constantly dragging us back down to earth. He challenges us stoic pilot types to dig deep, go all introspective, and ask ourselves, Are we really flying this airplane in the safest possible manner—by taking the human condition into account?

Even better, he uses poignant examples of said Human Factor that include Cap'n Kirk, Men in Black, and Superheroes like The Avengers. In short, he's my kinda pilot-writer! Ladies and gents, I give you: *The Pilot Factor*, by Jean Denis Marcellin!

Eric Auxier, aka Cap'n **Aux**
Captain, American Airlines
Author of *The Last Bush Pilots* and *There I Wuz!*
www.capnaux.com

It is possible to fly without motors, but not without knowledge and skill."

— WILBUR WRIGHT

Jean Denis Marcellin

TEAM DEFINITION

The concept & history of Crew

Resource Management

Not even a mile of visibility, and high gusting winds chasing snow around the airport in frenzied eddies of flurries and white powder. A typical winter day up north, with a strong low pressure system moving across and offering all sorts of challenges to anybody daring enough to go fly that day.

Was I daring? – or simply doing my job?... I pondered as I waited for the hangar door to open. I accepted the trip based on our company's SOPs (Standard Operating Procedures) and my own comfort level, knowing full well that although the ride would be rough, it would none-the-less be safe. I quickly found out that not everybody felt the same way. One of the paramedics, pulling me aside, pointed a finger at the winter storm blowing outside the open hangar door. "Just so you know" he stated boldly, "I do not feel comfortable going flying in this weather". And with this he stormed past me mumbling to himself, visibly upset by his apparently impending doom.

What was I to do? Good CRM (Crew Resource Management) would dictate that I take some time to communicate my thoughts clearly, and ensure that the "crew" – in this particular instance the paramedics – knew I was only doing my job. After all, I was confident in my weather and safety assessment of the trip. But an angry (and possibly scared) paramedic could also be a liability to any patient we might have to transport. I wasn't sure the "Good CRM" card would be sufficient. Why?

To understand this situation and question better, we first have to backtrack a little bit to the origins of CRM. In fact, let's go all the way back to the 1970s, and the birth of Human Factors.

The field of Human Factors focuses on "optimizing human performance and reducing human error. It incorporates the methods and principles of the behavioral and social sciences, engineering, and physiology. It is the applied science that studies people working together in concert with machines. It embraces variables that influence individual performance and variables that influence team or crew performance." [1]

It was around the 1970s that multiple high-profile accidents like the infamous Eastern Airlines crash into the Everglades [2] eventually prompted a new era into aviation psychology research. Investigators discovered that between 70% and 80% of aviation accidents involved human error rather than equipment failures or weather hazards. NASA's own studies regarding the subject found that the majority of crew errors consist of failures in **Leadership**, **Team Coordination**, and **Decision Making**.

The aviation community – under the umbrella of the ICAO (International Civil Aviation Organization) – decided to create an international standard to study and implement notions that would eventually become the core of aviation safety. They turned to psychologists to develop new kinds of psychological training for flight crews to face the new challenges they had just uncovered. That training focuses on **Group Dynamics**, **Interpersonal Communications**, and **Decision Making**. It is now known as CRM. [3]

Although CRM will be the focus of this book, it is important to understand that it is but one piece of the Human Factors puzzle. In fact, the ICAO now defines Human Factors through the SHELL model, typically known as the "building blocks" of Human Factors. [4]

Developed in the early 1970s along with the other aviation psychology research, SHELL – a conceptual model named after the initial letter of its components – helps us understand the relationships the human interaction with machines (Hardware), procedures (Software), the Environment, and each other (Liveware). [5][8][9]

The human element – or "Liveware" – is at the center of the SHELL model that represents a modern air operation system. It is the most critical component yet error-prone component in the system – interacting directly with the other parts constantly during each flight. [4] The following diagram illustrates the blocks representing the different components of Human Factors through the SHELL model.

(Picture Source: Atlas Aviation: The SHELL model[16])

Here are a few examples of the different parts in more details:

Software – the rules, procedures, written documents etc., which are part of the standard operating procedures.

Hardware – the aircrafts, their configuration, controls and surfaces, displays and functional systems.

Environment – the situation in which the L–H–S system must function, the social and economic climate as well as the natural environment.

Liveware – the human beings – the flight crew with other flight crews, controllers, engineers and maintenance personnel, management and administration people – within the system.

The SHELL model suggests the human is rarely, if ever, the sole cause of an accident[10]. We must then ask ourselves: why do 3 out of 4 accidents still result from performance errors made by two perfectly capable, skilled and trained crew?[11]

This is where CRM, or the Liveware->Liveware interface comes into play.

Defined by the ICAO[6] as the "interaction between central human operator and any other person in the aviation system during performance of tasks", the L-L involves interaction and interrelationships between individuals or groups. These interactions can influence behavior and performance positively or negatively. It includes[4][7]:

- interpersonal relations

- leadership

- crew cooperation, coordination and communication

- dynamics of social interactions

- teamwork

- Personality and attitude interactions

The study of the L-L interface and its challenges has been a key contributor in developing CRM programs and standards. Those standards aim at eliminating the potential errors or threats posed by the L-L interface mismatches. Some examples of such mismatches include:

- Communication errors due to misleading, ambiguous, inappropriate or poorly constructed communication. The Avianca Flight 52 is a vivid example, where communication was broken by language barriers between the crew and ATC, as well as poor communication between the crew - and ended in the untimely loss of an airliner.[15].

- Improper leadership, such as the story of First Air Flight 6560[16] where the captain refused to heed his first-officer's warnings, ultimately conducting a controlled flight into terrain and killing 12 people.

Now that we understand *where* the CRM concept comes from and *why* we need it, how do we define it?

Capt. Al Haynes was at the commands of the United Airlines Flight 232[17] on the ill-fated day where they sustained a total loss of flight control which ended with the crash of the airplane near Sioux-City, Iowa. Despite overwhelming odds, his exemplary use of CRM saved many lives.

He describes it as "a procedure and/or training in systems where human error can have devastating effects. Used primarily for improving air safety, CRM focuses on interpersonal communication, leadership, and decision making in the cockpit." [13]

I like this definition because it outlines both the strength and weakness of CRM. Although teaching CRM to professional pilots has done a tremendous job in reducing incidents related to poor interpersonal or leadership skills in the cockpit, it still has one major downfall: it's definition – and application – is tagged "cockpit only". Because it works by recognizing that a discrepancy between what is happening and what should be happening (often the first indicator that an error or threat is occurring) it only works as a reactionary tool most of the time. We teach that "Good CRM" will make managing airborne emergencies better. We teach that "Good CRM" will help the crew mitigate conflicts in the cockpit and thus reduce the chance for bad decisions, etc..

But I like to think that a flight doesn't start only when you go wheels up – and certainly does not end the moment you touch down. The operation of an airplane is one thing, but rendering services during the operation of an airplane is a whole other ball game. It includes not only the pilots, but also the rest of the team of professionals involved – from the cabin crew to the ramp workers, and so on.

This led me to question the true effectiveness of CRM on a global operational scale. True it strengthens cohesion within the cockpit crew, but what about the rest of the team? I was once asked how I would describe a good captain. The first image that came to mind was an orchestra conductor. As a team leader, a captain must know the music play by play, beat by beat. But he must also intrinsically trust every member of his team to do their own part with all the precision that their training and experience offers. If he is not in tune with every player in his team, then notes get lost and beats skipped... and the well-rehearsed symphony becomes cacophony.

THREAT AND ERROR MANAGEMENT (T.E.M.)

CRM has been taught, studied and is now a common notion for most flight crews around the world. So how can we further enhance its ability to not only mitigate errors, but also prevent them?

Modern CRM now takes a step back from the sole focus on Liveware->Liveware interaction, and brings back to view the "big picture" once more, giving the pilots the necessary tools to start acting and thinking preemptively rather than reactively.

In the early 90's, Delta Airlines and the University of Texas partnered together to create what is now most airlines' teaching standard: Threat and Error Management. [18]

Stemmed from LOSA – Line Operation Safety Audits, the joint research observed crews during training and regular line operation to identify:

- potential threats to safety;

- how the threats are addressed;

- the errors such threats generate;

- how flight crews manage these errors;

- specific behaviors that have been known to be associated with accidents and incidents.

In simpler terms, the resulting T.E.M. model is an overarching safety concept regarding aviation operations and human performance. It focuses on an important factor influencing human performance in dynamic work environments: the interaction between people and the operational context (the SHELL model).

T.E.M. now enables us to plan and actuate preventive measures, actively reducing the number of instances where CRM would be needed to mitigate a threat to safety. But how does it work? Here is how the team from the University of Texas describes their model:

"[...] risk comes from both expected and unexpected threats. Expected threats include such factors as terrain, predicted weather, and airport conditions while those unexpected include ATC commands, system malfunctions, and operational pressures. Risk can also be increased by errors made outside the cockpit, for example, by ATC, maintenance, and dispatch.

External threats are countered by the defenses provided by CRM behaviors. When successful, these lead to a safe flight. The response by the crew to recognized external threat or error might be an error, leading to a cycle of error detection and response. In addition, crews themselves may err in the absence of any external precipitating factor. Again CRM behaviors stand as the last line of defense. If the defenses are successful, error is managed and there is recovery to a safe flight. If the defenses are breached, they may result in additional error or an accident or incident"[18]

The failure of a crew to properly manage an error could result in an undesired aircraft state, the aircraft "being unnecessarily placed in a condition that increases risk. This includes incorrect vertical or lateral navigation, unstable approaches, low fuel state, and hard or otherwise improper landings. A landing on the wrong runway, at the wrong airport, or in the wrong country would be classified as an undesired aircraft state."[18]

There are three possible resolutions of the undesired aircraft state:

1. Recovery is an outcome that indicates the risk has been eliminated;

2. Additional error – the actions initiate a new cycle of error and management; and

3. Crew-based incident or accident.

Countermeasures to undesired states are a normal part of daily operations and aircraft systems. CRM is human performance training in the use and development of skills, knowledge and attitudes to act as three essential countermeasures: **Planning** (Managing anticipated and unexpected threats), **Execution** (essential for error detection and response) and **Review** (Managing changing conditions of a flight).

> *DID YOU KNOW?*
> *Empirical observations during training and checking suggest that as much as 70 % of flight crew activities may be countermeasures-related activities.*

OPERATIONAL APPLICATIONS

We have now come full circle, and the aviation industry is not only equipping pilots with the CRM tools, but with the full SHELL toolbox.

However, many challenges remain today. Even with the most in-depth studies and training, some barriers still oppose operational safety, more often than not imposed by social influences. Take for example the recent crash of Asiana 214, where the debilitating cultural and hierarchal rules placed the whole flight in jeopardy, tying the hands and effectively gagging the FO who seemed to be the only crew member with a correct situational awareness. His speaking up could have easily prevented an unnecessary accident. So in times of doubt, fall back to your basic training and Aviate – Navigate – Communicate. Through the use of proper CRM (Leadership, Communication and Decision Making), these basic actions will always remain the core of a successful, safe flight.

The T.E.A.M. idea takes a fresh look into CRM, allowing crewmembers to truly understand the variables involved inside AND outside of the cockpit, during all phases of the flight.

Threat & Error Assessment and Management defines the challenges faced by pilots in an airline or any operation offering flight services. It is crucial to first of all understand that the team does not only comprise the personnel onboard the aircraft during its mission, but anybody involved in the success of the mission. Taking the 3 main parts of a flight mission – Pre-flight; In-flight; Post-flight – I'll expand on the different aspects pilots must understand and foster to promote the highest safety and operational efficiency possible.

1) PRE-FLIGHT

-TEAM Assessment: EiQ; understanding your team's strengths & limits

-TEAM Communication: *Communication styles*

-TEAM Work: How your team's training will affect the success and safety of your flight

2) IN-FLIGHT

-TEAM Awareness: Situational awareness; identifying threats and errors

-TEAM Management: Leadership models & styles; managing threats and errors during flight

-TEAM Cohesion: Using all the available resources and personnel to ensure safety and success

3) POST-FLIGHT

-TEAM Review: The Secrets and Benefits of Debriefing

-TEAM Success: The Super-Hero Syndrome

Using this model, it is imperative to explore and understand the difference between Threats and Errors, what causes them and how to deal with them respectively.

I hope that after completing this study, pilots will be able to approach every flight with a better understanding of their responsibilities as well as the tools they can use to deliver performance and safety as a professional team, and not individual professionals.

REVIEW QUESTIONS

1. What do the 5 elements of the SHELL model stand for?

2. Using the SHELL model, describe in your own words why 70-80% of aviation accidents are attributed to human factors

3. What are the respective countermeasures to Threats, Errors and Undesired States are:

   1. Planning, Execution, Review

   2. Training, CRM, Skills

   3. Aviate, Navigate, Communicate

TEAM ASSESSMENT

EiQ; understanding your team's strengths & limits

Every journey begins with the discovery of self. It is the prologue to true self-awareness, and the cornerstone of the proverbial "people skills" that are critical to cohesive team operations in the ever changing and growing aviation industry.

The safety of every flight relies on the necessary knowledge of a multitude of different data, and the mastery of very demanding skills. But without the knowledge and mastery of one's own limits, emotions and mental state – the core foundation of safety is put in jeopardy. The human factor, the *Liveware*, is the center of the safety equation. This is where we start our study.

Every pilot I know has one thing in common: ego. It's a well-known fact – and if you are a pilot or work with pilots or even just happen to KNOW a pilot... you know I'm right! Be it a little or a lot, it is a part of who we are. It makes us accomplish brilliant things just as much as stupid – sometimes dangerous things. One funny thing I found about this particular fact is that the size of the ego is usually inversely proportional to the size of a pilot's experience.

This all became very clear to me one day. It actually literally got pounded into me. From the bottom of my seat. Hard to forget such a lesson! Here's an episode where the Liveware-Liveware interaction almost got me into "solid" trouble, and which reflects the need for a better understanding of this particular aspect of the SHELL model.

Still a fledging first officer on a beautiful state of the art airplane, with a powerful engine an lots of fun to offer, I was having the time of my life. The PC12 was an amazing aircraft to fly – even more so when you had the luxury of a clear VFR summer day to streak around the skies with no other care in the world. It was on such a day that we launched on a medevac call. Flying this leg, I leisurely took the airplane off the ground, enjoying the bright skies and the expectation of a few fun hours of flying. However, our secondary radio came alive just as we were leaving our home base airport's zone: "796, this is dispatch. Be advised the call is cancelled. Please return to base."

Bummer. Here goes my tanning session at Flight Level 250. Cancelling our IFR flight plan with center, we proceeded to turn around and prepare for landing. As we came in view of the field, my captain offered me a challenge. You know... It starts like "I bet you can't...". In this case, it finished with "land it RIGHT ON the numbers." Wait, what? Was he smoking something? On such a beautiful day, with almost no wind and a light aircraft to maneuver around. Would I ever show him. Lesson #1... never tell a pilot "I bet you can't" – especially if you really have a doubt he actually CAN! This being said, I took great care in my approach. Lining up the airplane just perfectly with the centerline, I started my descent on profile for the proposed touch down zone. However, I quickly realized that the few trees on short final for the runway would force me to keep a slightly higher descent profile than planned. Pursuing the challenge and trying to keep my ego safe, I continued without a remark.

Just before passing over the threshold, with clearly too much height left to lose to execute the challenge, my captain exclaimed, "Not going to make it!" That's right, rub it in! And so in a last ditch effort to save face, I let my nose down slightly to mitigate the flaring distance and touch down as close as possible to the target. What a mistake. Already coming in with a faster rate of descent due to the higher angle, that last decision set the aircraft on the runway with more force than I had ever felt. Following a VERY positive contact with the pavement, we found ourselves airborne again for a second, before I finally put the airplane back on the runway – with more care this time. Although I had a very forgiving crew and captain, I guarantee you I did not hear the end of this for months.

However, with the bad decision came some invaluable experience. I learned how vulnerable we are to peer pressure (or even ATC, management, or such) and how I react to people and stimuli around me. I also learned to place boundaries on my skill levels, and not exceed them unless I am in a training environment. Most of all, it really set the foundation for my understanding of Experience and the roles of emotional intelligence (EiQ) in a crew environment.

Experience can be defined in many ways. The universal definition of experience could be simply - Experience leads to good decisions. Bad decisions lead to experience. Makes sense, no? I like to describe experience as - A discovery of one's skills levels and ability to deal with stress and/or interpersonal relations.

How can we manage and assess threats or errors through the human factor? What tools do we have at our disposal to understand how personality or attitude problems are created or dealt with? How do we avoid bad decisions but yet enhance our team's strength?

The first step to solving – or avoiding a problem – starts with you. Or Me. It is crucial to understand here that in order for anybody to be able to solve a problem, he or she must first recognize it, and how he or she is affected by it. Once that is done, setting priorities and remedial actions becomes a lot easier.

Emotional Intelligence allows us to more clearly understand our relation and interaction with the problems as they become apparent, and thus more effectively deal with them. Pilots are trained to understand and deal with any problem that might arise with their airplanes, but seldom trained to understand the most complex machine: themselves. Safety can only be attained by combining proper training on both parts, in order to perform under diverse and/or adverse conditions.

"Emotional Intelligence is a way of recognizing, understanding, and choosing how we think, feel, and act. It shapes our interactions with others and our understanding of ourselves. It defines how and what we learn; it allows us to set priorities; it determines the majority of our daily actions."[1] There are five basic competencies that comprise the field of Emotional Intelligence. The first three are Intra-personal: they are invisible to others and occur inside of us. The last two are inter-personal: they occur between us and other people and are observable in our behavior. The better developed your intra-personal skills, the easier it is to demonstrate your inter-personal skills. [2] Daniel Goleman introduced EiQ as a focused set of five skills[3] that drive and enhance leadership.[4]

INTRAPERSONAL COMPETENCIES:

Can you identify your present mood? What are you feeling? How would you put in words your present mental state?

In *The 7 Habits of Highly Effective People,* the author describes the "ability to do what you just did as uniquely human. Animals do not possess this ability. We call it "self-awareness" or the ability to think about your very thought process.[5]

- **Emotional Self-Awareness** – Having the skill to focus your attention on your emotional state – being aware, in-the-moment, of what you're feeling. Are you stressed, excited, worried, or angry? Given that information about your emotional state, what should (or shouldn't) you do or say next? Use that information to help you make effective decisions to achieve better outcomes.

By being able to decipher one's emotional state also enables the person to clearly understand how their feelings affect their performance. Having established an accurate self-assessment, a person will then be able to recognize their strengths and weaknesses. Correct analysis of weaknesses will then enable learning from the mistakes or experience, and open the person to constructive criticism, different perspectives and self-development.

Confidence then becomes a natural byproduct of self-awareness. Being able to quickly assess their own ability to deal with any given situation, a pilot then gains the ability to project a stronger "presence" on the flight deck and in the team. They become more decisive under pressure and are also able to confidently voice options or opinions which might not always be "popular".

However, once the line is crossed to *over-confidence*, this ability can quickly become a threat to the team. Somebody who is too self-assured will tend to take rash decisions, not listen to others' opinions and react on a whim without thinking through the possible negative outcomes of some actions. You know, the good old "God Complex"... or what was it? Ego?

I have flown with many captains over the course of my career. I have learned a lot from each one of them, through positive *and* negative experiences. One lesson happened during my earlier days, flying a light Piper Chieftain over a mountainous range into a small strip. The airport was perfectly situated for any ski lovers flying into the area, but presented challenges to the pilots. On a particularly weather challenging day, the captain and I were assessing the options and trying to decide the safer way to proceed. He was one of those stronger-types personalities, and when you didn't agree with him, he was fairly hard to reason with. Wanting to save time, he suggested we fly right over the mountains, into IMC conditions and down the other side into the valley. When I suggested we could go around the mountain safely while remaining in VMC conditions, saving our passengers from a turbulent ride, he looked at me red-faced and exclaimed, "I AM the Captain. If you don't agree with me, you can go sit in the back with the passengers."

How was I to react to that? I was only trying to help, and my ego was truly hurt. The urge to go back with the passengers was strong, but trying to remain professional I nodded and kept my mouth shut. The short flight *around* the mountain, which the Captain eventually "deemed safer", felt like the longest in my life...

Never let your ego get the better of you, whether you are in charge or not. Think rational, act professional. Which brings us to:

- **Emotional Self-Regulation** – Self-regulation is about being able to manage disruptive emotions or impulses. The proverbial "cool-headed" composure, where a pilot can remain positive and focused, enabling him to think clearly through demanding and stressful moments.

Once a person has developed the skills to establish mastery over their own emotional state, they can then become a trusted and integral part of the team. Not only in situational management but also by demonstrating integrity and ethical behavior.

They also become stronger, reliable leaders who can be trusted to take the right decision, even if it's not the popular one, or confront members of the team who are being dysfunctional or disruptive to the safety of the operation.

Being able to understand and control one's emotions allows a team member to take responsibility for their own actions and decisions. This allows for a much deeper accountability process in the command hierarchy as well as peer-to-peer. It pushes the individual to meet their goals and commitments – safety and performance included.

Finally, a confident team member also becomes a tremendous asset to the team, as they now are able to adapt much more rapidly and seamlessly to new challenges. Always in control of themselves, any problem that might arise then becomes an opportunity to evolve, adapt or innovate – while managing stress and risk with always safety and performance in clear focus.

Be careful not to become jaded or unresponsive in times of need. Action is more often than not required to rectify or enhance a situation, and being too "calm" in the face of necessity would slow down your team and/or jeopardize safety when swift response is needed. Always keep an open and critical mind on every action, results and possible outcomes.

- **Emotional Self-Motivation** – This is the key, final ability which binds together the intrapersonal skills. It is about using your emotions to be positive, optimistic, confident, and persistent rather than negative, pessimistic and second-guessing yourself and your decisions.

Being able to recognize and act upon one's strengths and weaknesses, becoming confident in their own abilities to assess and manage situations enable pilots and other team members to truly achieve targeted performance and even go beyond set goals (safety, schedule, customer service, etc.).

Evolving from a purely reactionary standpoint to an action-based mind frame, a pilot is now able to set higher standards for the operation and lead the team safely towards an increased productivity without compromising their ability to deal with unforeseen circumstances. The increased efficiency of the individual and the team allows for better cohesion in stressful environments, as well as increased cognitive ability to gather and compile information – leading to better decision making – in turn mitigating risks and reducing "bad experiences". It turns the individual(s) into a results-oriented operation, able to evolve and learn in order to keep safety and performance at their peak.

With clear goals or target performance in mind, the individual or team is now ready to play an integral part in the success of the mission. Commitment becomes a natural derivative of this mind frame, pushing the person or team to accept self or group sacrifices to achieve their mission. From commitment stems initiative, providing results beyond the mission's goals and opening doors to opportunities otherwise unseen. From a single goal or set of goals (a successful flight for example), the team now becomes empowered with a vision and desire to pursue and achieve success outside of their "usual" duties, learning to manage situations and missions according to the company's global mission rather than the day to day set of normal operations.

A treacherous pitfall to be mindful of, however, is an overemphasis on target achievement rather than safety or other higher considerations. An on-time performance, for example, should never have more priority than the safe operation of the aircraft according to set regulations and common sense.

Rushing to Die[6] is the title of a poignant story about Singapore Airline Flight 006, a 747-400 that crashed during takeoff, from Taiwan on October 31, 2000[7].

The weather and winds were changing quickly due to an approaching typhoon. Fighting against time and weather, Flight 006's captain was rushing the departure to prevent being grounded by excessive crosswinds. He knew that missing the window of opportunity for departure meant returning to the gate and waiting for many hours before a chance to leave presented itself again. Angry passengers, exceeding flight duty times, extra costs and company retaliations were all factors he did not want to face. Instead, he rushed to depart, not reviewing the recent runway NOTAMs. He attempted to takeoff on a runway that was closed, dark and under construction, resulting in the loss of 82 lives.

Don't let your "sense of duty" jeopardize the life or well-being of those around you as well as yourself. If you are not the leader of the team, but recognize this situation, use the proper communication style as well as leadership style to help refocus the leader and team towards safety first, then targeted performance after.

INTERPERSONAL COMPETENCIES:

- **Social Awareness** – The ability to empathize, and recognize the differences and diversity of the team or customers.

Empathy is the first and most basic social skill needed to achieve social awareness. Not to be confused with sympathy – possessing the ability to listen effectively and accurately enough to put yourself in the other person's shoes. This is not necessarily to agree with them, but to truly understand the situation from their point-of-view in order to improve communication, problem-solving, and trust.

When able to properly empathize, individuals become skilled at anticipating and recognizing the needs of those around them. Be it the needs of the team, or the needs of the customers, this provides a tremendous asset to the team as they are now equipped to foresee possible problems which might arise and deal with them before they become a threat to the safety or targeted goal of the mission. When acting with initiative, true progress can be made towards a better customer experience or positive outcome for the team's success.

A correct understanding of the people around one's self also provides opportunities for mentoring and personal growth. When a leader is able to recognize a weakness or a potential for growth in an individual or the team, he or she is then able to foster that potential or address that weakness more easily, therefore impacting the potential of the whole team in a positive way.

After recognizing the potential in the individuals of the team, the leader is then able to focus and leverage on their diversity: assigning tasks based on individual strengths, hence reinforcing the ability of the team to face challenges, respond to needs, and achieve goals.

- **Social skills** – Through communication and action, demonstrate the ability to set a positive tone of cooperation no matter how difficult the situation or conversation and having other's best interests in mind while focusing on achieving goals to create positive outcomes.

To set the tone, the individuals of the team – and especially the team leader – must become skilled communicators. By communicating clearly and concisely their needs, problems, or ideas, team members enable the leader or the team as a whole to address and prioritize information to achieve the best outcome possible. Open communication fosters cooperation, which in turns provides the tools to reach the set goals and complete the given mission.

By effectively communicating goals or expectations, leaders gain the ability to inspire their team and enhance cohesion and cooperation, becoming catalysts for a shared vision or mission.

A skilled communicator also becomes better equipped to manage conflict resolution. While always promoting cooperation, they can recognize potential conflicts or defuse tense relations within the team by opening the communication and fostering collaboration towards a common goal, mission or vision – managing the balance between the focus on task and attention to stakeholder (internal or external) relations.

Finally, able communicators in the team become an important asset, providing the "bond" between members and driving the group synergy to achieve maximum potential and reach any given objective and challenges.

PERSONALITY VERSUS ATTITUDE

The importance of a well-balanced, emotionally aware and socially skilled person quickly becomes apparent when put in a team scenario. Any team member – including the leaders – have the potential to either become a problem or an asset. By understanding Emotional Intelligence (EiQ), a leader is able to assess the threat level or error potential of a team through the underlying intrapersonal traits of an individual or the interpersonal traits of the team. By doing so, you are then able to take corrective action before anything happens, thus reducing the margin of error and increasing the safety level of any operation as well as the success level of any mission or given goal.

When assessing your team or yourself, take care to clearly define the line between a person's attitude and his or her personality. According to the Flight Safety Foundation[8], "**personality** refers to stable patterns of behavior or persistent patterns of behavior that epitomize a person's interpersonal style and social interactions." In other words, personality is the Emotional Intelligence Quotient. We can measure it and analyze it, but it is not modified easily. It is often molded by your life experience and your social environment rather than a set of rules or training.

Where the leader can truly make an impact is by shaping the team's or individual's attitude. **Attitude** is referred to as "the combined belief, feeling and intended behavior toward safety. It can be changed by training and professional experience."[8]

So how does this all tie in together? How does this help us deal with problems in the cockpit in a safer or better way?

Well, as one of my favorite Captains of all time put it:

> *"The problem is not the problem. The problem is your ATTITUDE about the problem. Do you understand?"*
> *– Capt. Jack Sparrow*

Put simply, attitudes grow from assumptions of how things should be, which in turn are based on our perception of events or the people around us. The way we see things is the source of the way we think and the way we act. [5] Is the glass half full – or half empty?

Two people could be looking at the same identical facts, yet their perception, and thus their attitude versus the facts could vary widely, based on prior experiences. Our behavior, therefore, is a function of our decisions, not our condition or conditioning. The more aware we are of how biased or influenced our perception can be, the more we can take responsibility for our attitude, become more open minded and objective.

RESPONSE-ABILITY

Responsibility. The ability to choose our response. In view of the fact that our attitude is a function of our decisions, and not external influences, is it not then our responsibility to *choose* our attitude, one that reflects objectivity and clear priorities, rather than a product of our feelings or conditions?

This is the difference between what could be described as **Reactive** and **Proactive** people.

Reactive people are a product of their circumstances. Their feelings and emotions mirror their conditions, with little or no thought relative to their responsibilities. Proactive people, on the other hand, are driven by their values, and their keen self-awareness of their responsibilities, skills and potential.

Having the ability, then, also gives you the *responsibility* to choose right. Choose to prepare and train yourself and your team to understand, manage and enhance the individual or group EiQ level. Choose to be proactive, rather than reactive, and be driven by values and responsibility to safety rather than emotions and circumstances.

These choices will deeply impact the team's ability to manage challenges, problems or even daily operational goals. It will also **provide the ability to gain experience in a much more linear way**, reducing the necessary amount of risk involved to progress – in other words, tame the "learning curve" – and **increasing the reliability of each individual**.

Although this first glance at EiQ does not offer much more than a cursory approach to its inner workings and underlying operational importance, it is the very basis of every professional environment. Above learning professional skills, before even gaining general or technical knowledge, understanding and managing the true nature of one self and the human machine will provide a lasting foundation to any operation or team.

REVIEW QUESTIONS

1. Describe an instance where your emotional state dictated your actions or decision. Was it a controlled response?

2. What EiQ competency do you see as one of your strengths?

3. What EiQ competency do you see as one of your weaknesses?

4. Is iQ or EiQ more important in a cockpit? And why?

TEAM COMMUNICATION

The Four Communication Styles

The view outside the windshield gave the impression of a black abyss. It was late at night – close to 1am body time. The North Atlantic was keeping its secrets shrouded in the dark of the night, so they passed time talking of small things and trying to stay awake. The A330's cockpit was comfortable at least, and their destination was forecasting very welcoming weather.

Almost halfway across the ocean, however, the idyllic flight took a turn in a dramatic direction. Flashing harshly in the dim light of the cockpit, their computer's screen indicated some troubling news: a fuel imbalance on the #2 engine side had raised a flag. The captain, a 48 year old veteran pilot with countless hours under his belt, stared at the screen quizzically. Such a heavy imbalance could be the symptoms of a fuel leak, but he was fairly certain that the last few routine checks had not indicated such a problem or they would have caught it earlier. Those airplanes were so new and technology-dependent, he really did not trust the computer. Anyway, if the computer was so smart, it should be able to tell them about a simple fuel leak. It had to be a glitch.

The first officer, a much younger pilot of 28 years old, thought otherwise. Technology was part of his life, and he understood it well. He could almost communicate with machines. But today he was not running the show. After discussing and debating, the crew opted to start transferring fuel from one wing to another in order to try and "fix" the computer.

But something was not right. Now both tanks were losing fuel at a much higher rate than the engines' consumption was indicating. Despite the computer's dire predictions, the captain was convinced that it was only a "glitch" and the fuel tanks were well and full. The young first officer, sensing a rapidly approaching disaster, had to do something. But how could he communicate properly to his captain? Almost a lifetime of experience separated them, and a much different approach to technology and its usefulness. He had to get through to the captain, and make him understand how dire the situation was, get him to divert. And soon!

Finally changing course despite the captain's doubts, the flight headed towards a group of island along their way to Portugal. Minutes later, the #2 engine flamed out from fuel starvation, followed by #1 when all their fuel had bled dry. Thankfully, the FO's persistent efforts to communicate how perilous their situation was paid off. Their timely diversion had put them in gliding range of the Azores, where the crew of Air Transat Flight 236[1] safely landed after gliding their A330 almost 20 minutes, crossing 65 NM completely unpowered.

Communication is a broad skill. The Flight Safety Foundation[2] defines it as "the capabilities and limitations in transmitting information (speaking) and in receiving information (listening) using unambiguous (standard) phraseology to coordinate flight-deck activity and divide task loading, and to interpret correctly and act on information essential for task performance".

"One in four persons you meet will not get along well with you," my coworker told me one day. Really? I get along well with everybody! Mostly. "But," he added "I don't know why. I just heard it and thought it was an interesting statistic." Wait, you mean one out of four pilots I work with will cause me grief in the cockpit?

The reality is, I knew exactly what he meant. Human communication hinges on many variables, and the Liveware-Liveware link in the SHELL model highlights a very egregious part of the human factor which too often leads to incidents or accidents. Interpersonal styles, an individual's background, or even external influences can create barriers to clear communication. In Air Transat Flight 236's story, the junior first officer had to communicate with a much senior and, in reality, a much more experienced captain. He probably felt intimidated. Did that hinder their CRM and communication? A major communication error is represented in the "failure to respond to, or act on, a warning from another crew member."[2]

Did you know that, on average, verbal communication is only 30% effective? However – and thankfully – many tools are readily available today to help enhance our communication skills.

Imagine the one guy you really don't like seeing on the same line of the schedule. Maybe it is that he just talks and talks and by gosh you wish he'd get to the point sometimes and for once stop mentioning the POH! Or maybe he is just a bit rude and always has to be right. It could even just be that you can't stand their constant excited, "up-and-down" emotional roller-coaster. Or maybe he or she is just too nice and never has an opinion!

Any of these sound familiar? I'm guessing the answer is probably yes, in some way or form.

We all have our own experiences. They make us unique. Because of that, communicating with each other becomes a daily challenge. Shared experiences or training certainly make it easier. As professionals, where do we begin, what base can we use to build our communication skills on?

Pilots love rules of thumb. They make things easier to remember, and often time save us a lot of hassle trying to figure out some otherwise complicated equations. A great rule of thumb I found useful when studying communication is the four communication styles.

Joe Sharren [3] – a world leader in this subject – called them the four birds – Eagles, Owls, Doves and Peacocks. Each bird has a distinctive way to relate, to communicate. Although I've used the bird reference, these communications styles have been given many other names by other experts.

UNDERSTANDING THE FOUR COMMUNICATION STYLES

Another common name for it is the DISC method – Drivers, Influencers, Steadys, Compliants. Let's have a look at what they are and how knowing them can help you enhance your crew communication in the cockpit.

Driver (or Eagle)

The Eagle is easy to spot because they just want to get the job done. Get to the point, get results. Because of this, they can be perceived as bossy and insensitive. Extremely goal oriented, their major motivation is to get things done. They are also driven by recognition, and significance.

The Eagle paints with a broad brush and has little use for details, so when communicating with an Eagle, keep the verbal communication short and don't give them any more details than are absolutely necessary to get your point across. They don't like to acquire information. When information is needed, keep your verbal explanation short, then provide a detailed explanation through a nonverbal medium (email, paper, memo, etc.).

Their facial features are usually sharp, and they like to dress and maintain a 'clean cut' appearance. Eagles are comfortable in an environment that includes power and authority, freedom from supervision and working with a variety of activities. They also have trouble identifying with the team, and lack understanding of how powerful people working together can be.

The Influencer (or Peacock)

You know the Peacock...they're the life of the party and lots of fun. They love people and love to talk. Their natural sociability allows them to talk for long periods of time about almost anything. They have an attractive personality, are enthusiastic, curious, and expressive. Beware though, as they harbor the most volatile personality. Always interested in making a favorable impression on friends, coworkers and clients – their biggest fear and anger trigger is to lose face.

Peacocks are outgoing, exuberant and innovative. Outgoing and creative personalities have a difficult time doing bland tasks whether they are verbally or nonverbally communicated. Use a lot of examples, demonstrations and visual aids to effectively communicate with creative personalities. A creative mind will remember information by association.

Since they always see the best in people, Peacocks can have trouble making objective evaluations of people and situations. They don't like a lot of details and can appear a little disorganized. But we all benefit from people like them, who encourage us to open up and communicate. A Peacock contributes to a creative, outgoing and positive working environment.

The Steady (or Dove)

The person with a Dove communication style typically has a low key personality and is calm, cool and collected. They tend to be patient, well balanced and happily reconciled with life. Doves are the largest percentage of the population and they are typically competent and steady workers who do not like to be involved in conflict. When there is conflict they may be called upon to mediate the problem. They usually have many friends. One of their major motivations is to avoid offending anyone.

Doves facial features are usually soft, and they like to dress in whatever way is the most comfortable for them. Usually quiet, they are also extremely good listeners, thus sometimes providing some great ideas – but never wanting to make a decision.

Gentle, patient, understanding – they are part of the glue that keeps a team working together.

The Compliant (or Owl)

An Owl's life is made of facts. They love to gather details and organize things. Because their communication style includes a need for details, they sometimes hesitate to make decisions if they feel that they don't have enough facts. They love lists, charts, graphs and figures. They also have a habit of pointing out everything that can go wrong – but it's good to have Owls because they can see potential problems. An Owl needs to work with people who can help him or her see the big picture. A funny fact about owls – even while engaged in a simple thought process, they can appear to be 'mad' as their faces become stern. Don't worry, they are not mad at you – but simply thinking hard.

Owls like to finish everything they start. Their daily routine rarely changes; in fact, an Owl doesn't handle sudden changes well at all. But their love of routine can slow things down in an environment that requires quick decisions and action – an airplane cockpit being one of them.

EAGLE	PEACOCK
⁑ Goal Oriented	⁑ Sociable
⁑ Needs to see results	⁑ Enthusiastic, impulsive
⁑ Quick reaction time, decisive	⁑ Future Oriented
⁑ Independent	⁑ Conceptual, Innovative
⁑ Practical	⁑ Egotistical
⁑ Direct	⁑ Needs to be accepted by others
⁑ Controlled facial expressions	⁑ Undisciplined

OWL	DOVE
⁑ Fact Oriented	⁑ Personal security, acceptance
⁑ Needs to be accurate	⁑ Cooperative
⁑ Organized, systematic	⁑ Personable
⁑ Slow reaction time	⁑ Enthusiastic, Loyal
⁑ Serious, industrious	⁑ Perceptive
⁑ Methodical, Tenacious	⁑ Hates conflict
	⁑ Prefers to work in teams

Very diplomatic with people, they use a critical approach to analyzing performance and don't take criticism personally. Sit down with a person who is detail-oriented and spend time verbally going over every task, expectation and purpose. Allow for questions between each instruction because detail-oriented personality types will typically ask a lot of questions to ensure they accurately understand what is being communicated.

Qualities and Characteristics of each Birds

How do you relate to your fellow birds, while caged in the same cockpit for a day or more? The model's rule of thumb indicates that we most often have a Primary and Secondary communication style.

By understanding the basic differences and how to relate to your fellow pilot, you will be able to avoid a tremendous amount of conflict simply linked to misunderstandings and communications barriers.

Although emotional intelligence might be called the "foundation" of any team or individual - communication is an essential part in the potential for success or failure. For a team or individual to achieve their goal, interaction will always be present. Be it in communicating with team members or stakeholders, a skilled person will remove the risk for misunderstanding of goals or needs, thus reducing the margin of error which could introduce safety problems or the inability to complete the mission down the line.

Pilots are often entrusted with a leadership role – but the responsibility is not theirs alone. Cabin crew and support personnel also hold an irrevocable place in the team leadership and provide key skills for success. Clear and effective communication between all the groups and within each sub-group must then be amongst the top priority and skill-set of each TEAM member.

FACTS	PEACOCK	EAGLE	DOVE	OWL
How to Recognize:	Get excited	Like their own way; decisive & strong viewpoint	Like positive attention, Need be helpful & regarded warmly	Want a lot of data, ask many questions. Methodical & systematic
Tends to Ask	**Who?** (the personal dominant question)	**What?** (the results oriented question.)	**Why?** (the personal non-goal question.)	**How?** (the technical analytical question.)
What They Dislike:	Boring explanation. Wasting time with too many facts.	Wasting time debating rather than acting	Rejection, impersonal treatement, uncaring attitudes.	Making an error, being unprepared, spontaneity.
Reacts to Pressure and Tension By:	"Selling" their ideas, arguments.	Taking charge taking more control.	Becoming silent, withdraws, introspective.	Seeking more data & information.
Best way to Deal With:	Get excited with them. Show emotion.	Let them be in charge.	Be supportive; show you care.	Provide lots of data & information.
Likes To Be Measured By:	Applause, feedback, recognition	Results, Goal-oriented.	Friends, close relationships .	Activity & busyness that leads to results.

FACTS	PEACOCK	EAGLE	DOVE	OWL
Must Be Allowed To:	Get ahead quickly. Likes challenges.	Get into a competitive situation. Likes to win.	Relax, feel, care, know you care.	make decisions at own pace, not cornered or pressured.
Will Improve With:	Recognition & some structure with which to reach the goal.	A position that requires cooperation with others.	A structure of goals & methods for achieving each goal.	Inter-personal and communi-cation skills.
Likes to Save:	Face. They will do or say anything to come out looking good.	Time. They like to be efficient, get things done now.	Relationship & Friendship means a lot to them.	Mistakes. They hate to make an error, be wrong or get caught without enough info.
For Best Results:	Inspire them to bigger & better accomplishments.	Allow them freedom to do things their own way.	Care & provide detail, specific plans to be completed.	Structure a framework or "track" to follow.

REVIEW QUESTIONS

1. Looking back at the 4 birds, which one(s) do you relate to the most?

2. Which ones do you find you understand or relate to the least?

3. Have you ever felt uncomfortable around a certain type of people, not knowing why?

4. Do you think knowing more about the communications styles can help you relate better or more efficiently to those around you?

TEAM WORK

*Your team's training will affect the
success and safety of your flight*

> *"Without Knowledge, Skill cannot be focused. Without Skill, Strength cannot be brought to bear and without Strength, Knowledge may not be applied"*
> *— Alexander the Great's Chief Physician*

The untimely tragedy of the Air France Flight 447[1] has left the aviation community baffled, and later scandalized over the shocking revelations shared by the investigation. What went wrong? A perfectly airworthy airplane, with two perfectly working engines, ended up lost for years and became one of the greatest mysteries of aviation. With answers, however, came more questions, and as pilots all over the world tried to make sense of it all, the dreadful truth came out: the lack of training on a procedure as seemingly simple as a stall recovery led to the 3 minutes of horror and untimely demise of all the souls on board of flight 447.

A few years later, another tragedy puzzles the world of aviation. Despite the striking resemblance with the Air France Flight 447 story, Colgan Air Flight 3407[2] highlights a completely different and inherent problem with the world of commercial aviation. Although the NTSB attributed the crash and death of all the people on board the Dash 8 Q400 commuter to pilot error and more importantly poor training, Colgan Air responded to the NTSB report in a letter: "They [the pilots] knew what to do in the situation they faced that night a year ago, had repeatedly demonstrated they knew what to do, and yet did not do it. We cannot speculate on why they did not use their training in dealing with the situation they faced." And so, despite recurrent training and demonstrated knowledge of the necessary skills, the crew of Colgan Air Flight 3407 failed to perform the critical yet simple stall-recovery maneuver which would have resulted in a safe outcome.

The same year as the Colgan Air accident, another airliner crashed near New York City. But against all odds and while quickly running out of options, the legendary Captain Chesley Sullenberger accomplished the extraordinary and ditched his Airbus A320 in the Hudson River after a total power loss following a fatal bird-strike. His training, knowledge, and above all – clock-work precision in his performance – saved the lives of all the souls on board the airplane and resulted in no fatalities onboard US Airways Flight 1549[3]. The Guild of Air Pilots and Air Navigators awarded the entire flight crew of Flight 1549 a Master's Medal[4]. The medal is awarded rarely, and only for outstanding aviation achievements.

"The reactions of all members of the crew, the split second decision making and the handling of this emergency and evacuation was 'text book' and an example to us all. To have safely executed this emergency ditching and evacuation, with the loss of no lives, is a heroic and unique aviation achievement. It deserves the immediate recognition that has today been given by the Guild of Air Pilots and Air Navigators." - *Master of the Guild.*

In the light of these events and reports being made available to the aviation community, a question remains. What can we – as pilots – learn and apply in our own jobs, every day, every flight? The truth is simple:

TRAINING + PERFORMANCE = SAFETY.

Captain Fantastic[5] is the title given by the media to Richard de Crespigny, the captain who saved 466 lives on failed Qantas flight QF32. He safely landed his crippled Airbus A380 after losing two engines and many critical systems due to a catastrophic turbine explosion.

De Crespigny mentioned in an interview afterwards[6], "While landing the plane, we had to deal with more than 60 separate system failures. The wing was cluster-bombed. The aircraft had phenomenal damage in all systems."

It's easy to see why he was awarded such a title. But the reason behind the safe landing of QF32 was how the captain and his crew handled the emergencies. "It was a flight that you could never train for. You might practice one or two emergencies, not 60," continues de Crespigny. So what was their secret? "I was supported by an extraordinary crew with lots of experience." Their "flying background, check and training culture, automation and simulation, [and] human factors"[7] all came together in the time of greatest need.

Sadly the story is not the same everywhere. In this modern world of technology, one is often prone to relying on the available tools to complete the required tasks at hand. A brand new airliner like the A380 offers so many safety redundancies, performance-enhancing tools and reduced-load management systems that it is now technically feasible to train a pilot from ab-initio to the right seat of an airliner without having the pilot pay his proverbial dues flying smaller aircraft to gain experience first. But where does this leave us?

MacLean's Magazine published a cover story called *Cockpit Crisis*[8], relating to the number of high profile incidents and accidents in the airline industry pertaining to pilot training. With the rapid growth of the airline business in the world and the plethora of low-cost carriers opening their doors to brand new pilots, what can we do to ensure a constant reliability in the training of the new pilots? One of my favorite quotes, and I wish I knew who said it - *"We do not rise to the level of our expectations. We fall to the level of our training."*

But what if, in some instance – like the Air France 447 crash – training is not enough? Sometimes, there are truly no substitutes for experience. The head of the Air Canada Pilot Union tells MacLean's in *Cockpit Crisis*, "It almost never happens in real life like it happens in a simulator. It's almost never textbook in my experience. You practice it one way and when something finally does happen, it's always way more nebulous and insidious. [...] There's something that you just can't simulate," he says. "It's gained through experience."

Training does not only include pages of a manual, or the simulator sessions. Training also includes a strong commitment to developing and maintaining a high standard of safety, and a complete commitment to Crew Resource Management – which involve all the aspects of multi-crew and TEAM-based decisions and actions. The industry is slowly shifting pace, understanding the true value of the individual behind the title. A pilot is a pilot is a pilot. A crew-member, however, truly takes part in the synergy of the team work, and the symbiotic environment of the technology versus man. Next time you climb in the cockpit of an airplane, ask yourself this question: are you ready, capable and properly trained to deal not only with the airplane you operate, but also with the crewmembers in your team? Once CRM mentality is ingrained in a pilot, one mission is accomplished. The next step is imparting the proper knowledge and skills to make sure that in any situation that might arise, the pilots are ready to perform and exceed standards and expectations.

PURSUING EXCELLENCE

Once training is completed, it is the duty of all pilots to perform up to the standards established by the training establishment, regulating agency and their employer. Performance, however, can be affected by a number of factors which may or may not be in control of the pilot or the employer. For example: Stress and fatigue are two main players in the performance abilities of a pilot.

Going back to the TEM (Threat and Error Management) model, it's now easy to see where threats might arise and become an issue to the safety of flight.

Whether they stem from a situation outside of work or are induced by a high-workload or schedule, stress and fatigue for example will often be present in a pilot's environment. The ability to understand, recognize and deal with those factors are both the pilot's *and* the employer's responsibility.

A pilot should know his or her limit and refuse to fly in an overtired state. Did you know that after 17 hours of sustained wakefulness cognitive psychomotor performance decreases to a level equivalent to the performance impairment observed at a blood alcohol concentration of 0.05%. If you get pulled over with this amount of blood alcohol concentration, you *will* be charged for driving under the influence. After 24 hours of sustained wakefulness cognitive psychomotor performance decreased to a level equivalent to the loss of performance observed at a blood alcohol concentration of roughly 0.10%. You are effectively ***flying drunk***.

Other key factors in performance include emotions and relationship-induced stress. By this I mean the synergy between you and your crew members, and how well you adapt and work with different personalities and characters. It is very important at this stage for a pilot to be completely aware and in control of their own reactions. To help with this, a lot of resources have recently been made available concerning Emotional Intelligence, and what it means in a high-stress, high-demand team environment. The Institute for Health and Human Potential offers a short free online test which allows you to understand your own reactions to the events and people around you, and thus readjust them in a way which will increase performance during the operation of an airplane. Remember: Lack of performance degrades safety. Whether it's stress, fatigue, or otherwise induced, it plays a crucial role in the operations every day.

Threats are real, and ever present. They can be external, but they often also come from ourselves – the very center of the SHELL model. One of those internal threats is Human Error.

When a crew is able to use their training to maintain a proper performance level, the safety factor of the flight increases exponentially. The higher the skill level, the less error-prone we become. Training starts with your first step in flight school, and never stops for the rest of your career. Be it every two years, yearly or even every 6 months, you will be required to train and demonstrate proper knowledge and skill levels. But aside from that which is imparted to us during recurrent training, it is also our duty, as pilots, to maintain this level between training periods and remain able to perform, just as Captain Sullenberger did, with clock-work precision. **Remember**, practice doesn't make perfect. *Perfect practice makes perfect.*

Of course, nothing will ever replace experience, but strict adherence to set procedures and a high level of system knowledge will more often than not get you out of a sticky spot. However, although focusing on avoiding errors is helpful and will often help find and trap problems before they happen, it is a limiting objective. We are only human, and no matter how good we get, we will always have errors when operating and managing a complex airplane and cockpit environment. So what should be our objective, if not to avoid errors and perform safely?

ACHIEVING EXCELLENCE

"Achieve Excellence, don't just avoid Errors", should be the new mantra for all pilots and operators.

Never forget that you have responsibility over your life and the souls onboard your airplane. Accidents can happen at any time and constant vigilance and due-diligence is obligatory for every crew member aboard an aircraft. This means doing your best, every day and every flight, to sharpen your skills, broaden your knowledge, so that you can perform, even when terror strikes – and bring one, two, or even hundreds of lives to safety. Train, Perform, Stay Safe. By aiming for excellence and not simply error avoidance, we become pro-active instead of reactive, and can now focus on the bigger picture at work, or, in other word, on our situational awareness.

> *"Your work is to discover your work and then with all your heart to give yourself to it."* – Buddha

REVIEW QUESTIONS

1. Complete the sentence:

Practice doesn't make _____.

Perfect _____ makes perfect.

2.   What   "formula"   can   be   used   to   describe   flight   safety?

_____ + _____   =   Safety

3. What should be the pilots' mantra?

   Achieve _____, don't just avoid _____.

4. In your opinion, what is the greatest tool or improvement to safety in aviation?

TEAM AWARENESS

Situational Awareness; Identifying

Threats & Errors

Another flash. The night seemed like day for a fraction of a second, as light streaked through the sky. As we raced between clouds and rain, it was hard to tell how far – or how close – it had been. Looking back on the night, it really hadn't started badly. But it still held a few surprises for us...

With every mile flown we were getting closer to the heart of the storm. But every minute passing also took us closer to the airport. Staring intently at the GPS map, where the weather radar was overlaying a grim picture, my first officer's voice broke the silence sporadically as he answered ATC commands while they vectored us around for the ILS approach. I had wished to land straight in and avoid any time we didn't have to spend near those thunderstorm cells, but the winds forced us to fly around to the other side of the airport. At least it gave us the use of a precision approach rather than the VOR alternative. Still, this didn't seem to inspire confidence to my fledgling FO. "Fun time eh?" he managed to say with a weak smile. I returned the smile, but my mind was racing.

Our small cockpit was teeming with action. Every turn brought us closer to our final vector, and closer to a thunderstorm cell. Almost on a regular rhythm, the sky lit up around us, brighter and brighter each time. We HAD to land soon – or turn around. But something was wrong...

The controller, in his haste to help us land and trying as best he could to keep us away from the towering cells of raging storm just aside of our course, had put us very close to our final approach course. Too close in fact – I realized – as I kept mentally calculating our descent angle and current altitude. We would miss the glideslope which we'd hoped would take us safely to the runway. If that happened, a missed-approach would most likely be needed and we'd miss our only opportunity to land at this airport, forcing us to divert and cancel the mission. I couldn't take that chance.

Between two short communications and the preparation for the approach, I quickly explained the situation to my FO: "If we don't get lower NOW, we're probably not going to be stabilized going down the ILS, and the weather is reported to be pretty low. Ask the controller for a descent or we'll miss the glide-slope!"

His look told me he understood plain as day. "ATC, this is MEDEVAC 101, we..uhm.. we need a descent NOW.... uhm.. please!" "Medevac 101, turn left heading 280. You are cleared for the ILS approach 25."

That's all we needed to hear. "Set the glide-slope intercept altitude!" I asked, all the while reaching for the vertical speed control button. Almost as fast as a lightning flash, we started making our way down as we veered to intercept our final approach course. While the aircraft captured the localizer and turned inbound for the final approach, the glide-slope slid into place and, with it safely captured, we made our way down and landed, happy, tired, grinning. "Fun times indeed!" I finally replied, almost laughing in relief.

SITUATIONAL AWARENESS

Every story carries a lesson. The message here is Situational Awareness. If I could speak of any tool more precious than anything else in flight, this would be it. Countless accidents can be attributed to the crew losing their situational awareness. From a burnt light-bulb (Eastern Air Lines Flight 401[1]) to black-hole illusions, to fatigue and poor training (Colgan Air 3407[2]), the reasons are more numerous than you can imagine. Far too often an accident and loss of lives could have been avoided by a better crew coordination in the cockpit when faced with stressful or even sometimes mundane circumstances.

Situational awareness (SA) involves being aware of what is happening around you, in order to understand how information, events, and your own actions will impact goals and objectives, both immediately and in the near future. An individual with good situational awareness generally understands better how people, machines and their environment can or should interact to create the desired outcome. Lacking or inadequate situational awareness has been identified as one of the primary factors in accidents attributed to human error.[3]

In simple words, Situational Awareness is:

- The perception of the elements in the environment within a volume of time and space

- The comprehension of their meaning and

- The projection of their status in the near future.

As crews train together and fly, it is crucial and imperative that they learn to communicate clearly. This in turn provides the channel necessary for basic information to travel back and forth, for example. Who is flying the aircraft? Where is the aircraft in relation to the targeted flight path or approach? What is the actual configuration or desired configuration for this phase of flight? Many details have led to unfortunate errors, simply because of assumptions or even tunnel vision – focusing all the attention and resources on a problem rather than the flight itself. It is then a priority that the entire team share the situational awareness and communicate sufficiently to ensure complete cohesion.

THE SWISS CHEESE MODEL

In order to facilitate aircraft accident investigation, James Reason proposed in 1990 a revolutionary model, which would come to be known today as *The Swiss Cheese Model*[4].

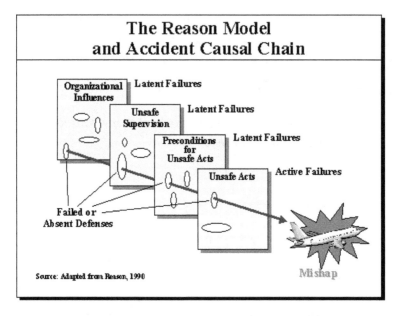

It became widely popular and useful. Forcing investigators to work backwards from the proverbial *active failure*, the direct cause of many accidents, it brought to view the many *latent failures* which influenced the outcome along the way.

But how does this tie in with SA? The three levels of latent failures – Preconditions for Unsafe Acts , Unsafe Supervision, and Organizational Influences – speak volume as to the effects of insufficient situational awareness.

In the case of Air France 447, the pilot's inaction or inability to recover from the stall condition was the direct cause of the crash. But many factors came into play which, had they been more aware of, could have saved their lives. The Precondition for Unsafe Acts part was played through their failure to recognize the change in the computer's logic as well and to interpret the flight instruments properly. But why did they miss all those clues?

Unsafe supervision could be seen where two fairly junior pilots were at the helm when they encountered some very challenging weather.

Should they have woken up the captain? Should the captain have been more aware of the weather ahead? A better understanding of the challenge and their own skill level could have saved their lives.

Taking a step back further, we also realize that there was a latent failure in their training. Without having the knowledge of how to deal with such a situation, it was hard for them to use this skill. Organizational influences, however far back in the chain, also had their part to play.

Although the pilots' immediate lack of situational awareness spelled their doom, it is clear that along the way many other people had a lack of vision, a lack of situational awareness which could have stopped this tragedy in its track. This leads us to the concept of Team SA.

TEAM SITUATIONAL AWARENESS

The United Airlines Flight 173 crash in 1978 is by far recognized as one of the major contributors to the birth of CRM. It highlighted many issues that are now the main objects of every Human Factors or Crew Resource Management training.

The NTSB determined the following probable cause[5]:

"The failure of the captain to monitor properly the aircraft's fuel state and to properly respond to the low fuel state and the crewmember's advisories regarding fuel state. This resulted in fuel exhaustion to all engines. His inattention resulted from preoccupation with a landing gear malfunction and preparations for a possible landing emergency."

The NTSB also determined the following contributing factor:

"The failure of the other two flight crewmembers either to fully comprehend the criticality of the fuel state or to successfully communicate their concern to the captain."

Despite the fact that some of the crew members may have understood what was going on, this was not enough to save the flight. Team SA is then the next step in achieving safety and performance, as every member needs to be aware and cognitive of what is going on around them.

In other words, Team SA is defined as "the degree to which every team member possesses the SA required for his or her responsibilities" [6]. The success or failure of a team depends on the success or failure of each of its team members. If any one of the team members has poor SA, it can lead to a critical error in performance that can undermine the success of the entire team. By this definition, each team member needs to have a high level of SA on those factors that are relevant for his or her job. It is not sufficient for one member of the team to be aware of critical information if the team member who needs that information is not aware.

So what are simple ways to prevent Team SA from failing?

- Anticipate the needs of other team members.

- Adapt to task demands efficiently.

Each team member has a pertinent goal to their specific role, relevant to the overall team goal. To achieve their individual goal however, they need to be aware of certain parameters relevant to the whole team. Team SA, therefore, can be represented as shown below [7]. As the members need each other to meet the overall team goal, some overlap between each member's individual goals and their situational awareness requirements will be required. CRM is described as the team's ability to match their tasks in a coordinated effort to reach a common goal. That coordination may occur as a verbal exchange, a sharing of displayed information, or by some other means.

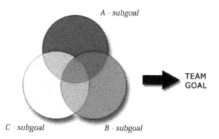

Now, before we get carried away, let's go back to basics. Remember that little adage you learned in flight school?

AVIATE. NAVIGATE. COMMUNICATE.

Let me rephrase that in different words.

Always fly the plane first. No matter where you are or who is talking to you, the aircraft, despite all the automation now available to flight crews, is only a machine. Granted, some aircraft are "smarter" machines but the pilot should ALWAYS be in positive control of the aircraft. The famous "What's it doing now?" question should be the prime target of any flight crew, eliminating any doubt as to whether or not the flight crew is in control, and if not, what needs to be done immediately to regain full control of the aircraft. YOU are in control, not the FMS, not even ATC. If your FMS takes you on the unprotected side of a hold, or your autopilot takes you down below minimums when a go-around was predicated, who will take the blame? For this step, communication between the crew is the key to success and safety.

Once positive control has been ascertained, making sure that you are not headed unwittingly toward a situation where your aircraft could end up losing a limb (CFIT, thunderstorms, etc) is your next priority. Understand the dynamics of the weather you are encountering and always make sure to have an egress route if needed. For example, if you are encountering freezing rain and know it's associated with a warm front, you will be ready to ask for a climb if needed to get away from it. Thunderstorm weather is often hard to predict as it can develop so fast, but a good knowledge of the area's weather trends can give you a better awareness of where to expect it and how to avoid it best. Prepare as much as you can before you leave, and get updates as often as necessary on the weather to avoid being trapped. As you navigate en-route or on an approach, always cross check available information to confirm the correct position and required configuration.

Finally, broadcast your needs or intentions as often as possible. ATC is there to help and will often try to work with pilots in order to facilitate time constraints or safety matters. You've already setup clear communication in the cockpit, so the PM should have no problem relaying the information or requests to ATC, or vice versa, always keeping the Pilot Flying informed of what's going on outside the airplane. Information such as conflicting traffic, changing weather conditions or special procedures to expect are crucial pieces of information which should be shared in a timely manner, but never taking precedence over flying the aircraft or navigating safely.

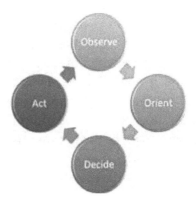

In short, "to aviate, navigate and communicate, you must be aware of the **plane**, the **path**, and the **people** (crew, passengers, dispatchers, and air traffic controllers). Not only do you need to monitor and evaluate these three things now, but you need to **anticipate** what's going to happen in the future and also **consider** contingencies. The current and future state of the plane, the path, and the people are the components of the plan."[8]

A very effective tool to help crews retain sharp situational awareness is the OODA Loop[9]. Used by the Air Force and Special Forces today, it is a simple acronym based on four simple concepts: **O**bserve; **O**rient; **D**ecide; **A**ct.

The *loop* is a visual[10] concept involving the idea of a dynamic circle, constantly present in the pilots' decision-making process. It clearly reflects the need for a strong situational awareness as the base for good decision-making.

Remember, it is always when the order of things is upset that an accident will occur. If a crew is busy discussing an approach procedure and forgets to bring the power up when the autopilot levels off after a descent, the imminent stall will be a much graver danger than the possible deviation to a procedure. At the same time, an untimely communication can distract the crew from a crucial part of their procedure, missing a descent step down on an approach and quickly creating confusion or worse...

Fly. Track. Talk.

Plane. Path. People.

In times of need, restructure your team's focus around the basics. If you ever feel like you've lost situational awareness, aim for the nearest Stable, Simple and Safe situation. Communicate with your crew and ATC to better recover the *Big Picture.* Ensure that each member is targeting key goals, while working as a cohesive unit to promote safety and a successful mission.

REVIEW QUESTIONS

1. SA Consists of what 3 elements?

   1. Perception, Comprehension, Projection

   2. Software, Hardware, Liveware

   3. Maintenance, Design, Weather

   4. None of the Above

2. Describe an event where you feel the "Swiss Cheese Model" was happening, and multiple latent failures were leading towards an active failure. What did you do to stop it?

3. What was done to prevent any further occurences?

4. What is the key to successful SA?

   1. Aviate, Navigate, Communicate

   2. Plane, Path, People

   3. Fly, Track, Talk

   4. All of the Above?

TEAM MANAGEMENT

Leadership models and styles;
Managing threats and errors
during flight

"Management is doing things right. Leadership is doing the right thing."
- Peter Druker and Warren Bennis

I think one of the most famous leaders of all times, and one to which most pilots can relate, is Capt. James T. Kirk, of the USS Enterprise. I can remember watching my first Star Trek movie as a boy, entranced by the music, and in awe of the crew and its mission, "To Boldly Go where no one has been before". Episode after episode, movie after movie, Captain Kirk never ceased to amaze, always successfully leading his team out of harm's way and winning over his foes, either by wits or cunning. His was the quintessential leader: Charismatic, knowledgeable, bold, unwavering yet dedicated to his crew to a fault.

On the other hand, you have Michael Scott (Steve Carell), manager par excellence of the well-known and much loved American sitcom *The Office*. Always (almost always...) calm, and dealing daily with micro-crisis, interpersonal challenges and the daily routine of their work, Michael is the modern image of the manager. Although far from perfect, he does reflect many qualities and face the many challenges of the modern day professional teams.

Now try imagining Michael on the deck of the Enterprise, trying to replace James Kirk on his sick day. Aside from looking good in the uniform (the uniform makes everybody look good!), his inability to make game changing split second decisions during crisis moments would have spelled the doom of the Enterprise many times over. Perhaps he could have managed a level of the ship more aptly than anybody else, but inspiring the crew to go boldly where nobody went before would have been... limited. Now Kirk is in *The Office*, trying to deal with deadlines for paper deliveries and micro managing the employees' relations would have driven him to madness, looking for the first opportunity to release a photon torpedo on the first target of opportunity!

As pilots, and especially as Captains, the responsibility to play both acts as a single entity can become demanding and becomes ever more challenging as the scope of the operation increases. The team members are not always confined IN the aircraft – think ground crew, dispatch, etc. So it is crucial that the two different roles be well defined in order for us to provide the highest performance possible as well as best customer service.

The manager is the base of a cohesive team (whether it be the CEO, Chief Pilot or Captain) who must clearly define everybody's roles, goals, and performance standards. By doing so, it provides a smooth operation of regular tasks, and mitigates the risk of pre-asserted threats. In order to reach to performance standards, technical training is crucial to provide the proper skill basis.

In Aviation for example, those skills would relate to the direct flying of the aircraft by the flight crew, or proper management of the cabin environment by the cabin crew. To assist the crew and promote a homogenized cockpit environment, Standard Operating Procedures become a must-have for every team.

> *"Management is about skills, leadership is about skills coupled with character."*
> *-Patrick and Joan Gebhardt[2]*

Leadership takes a well-managed team and evolves it into a well-oiled machine. It allows team members to take the initiative and promotes innovation, all the while being conducive to a better client experience. Once the team reaches this level, technical skills become less relevant, and interpersonal skills as well as the individuals' character will be the key to the team's success.

" Leaders are needed most where people interaction is highest, be it among employees or in between customers and employees" -*Business or Pleasure*

Another way to distinguish the differences between Management and Leadership is by looking at the way our brains function. In his much-acclaimed book *The 7 Habits of Highly Effective People*, Stephen Covey describes **Leadership** as "primarily a high-powered function, right brain activity. It's more of an art; it's based on a philosophy". He continues on to explain **Management** as "the breaking down, the analysis, the sequencing, the specific application, the time-bound left brain."

In his words: "Manage from the left; lead from the right."

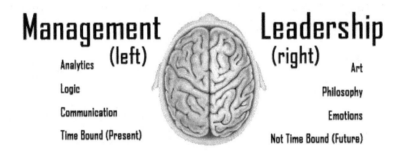

Management (left)
Analytics
Logic
Communication
Time Bound (Present)

Leadership (right)
Art
Philosophy
Emotions
Not Time Bound (Future)

Now that the foundation has been laid, let's take a deeper look at Managing versus Leading your team.

THE MANAGER

Management types are generally divided into 5 categories(3). Further research will show that aside from management types, management style also comes in effect, adding complexity to the equation. Which one are you? More importantly, is there an "ultimate" type?

Autocratic:

A manager using this type leaves little to questioning. He sets out goals, seeking no input from the rest of the team. This type holds no interest in individual achievement or satisfaction – only the required targeted performance to achieve the goals. There is little or no input allowed from the team members. This "dictatorship" type of management promotes discipline in high-stress environments or situations, but it can rapidly deteriorate the team's performance or safety when the manager refuses to take valuable input from team members at critical moments. However, it can be valuable with lower-skilled teams, offering structured guidance until the team or individual reaches their potential. In short, it is great for immediate threat-mitigation and reduces the overall error potential of a low-skilled team.

In Aviation, it can sometimes be related to the "old school" captains, deeming themselves "god" in their aircraft and leaving no room to comment or question their authority. CRM has helped crews understand over time that this type can be good as well as bad, and why.

Two good examples of autocratic management gone "good" or "bad" can be found in aviation. Two very critical moments, where captains using the same management types had two opposite outcomes: one saved lives, the other lost lives. Can you guess?

Captain Sully successfully glided and ditched his Airbus after a double engine failure following a bird strike. Time was against him, and he quickly made a decision which ended up saving countless lives. Do you think he had time to ask around for options or opinions? Taking command of the aircraft, he provided an even-handed management of the situation, providing a positive outcome for the rest of his team to lead the survivors to safety.

30 years prior to that, a much different outcome came from the same management type. 1977, Tenerife was the theater of one of the most devastating aircraft tragedies in flying history. But could it have been avoided? Definitively! The KLM captain, a high-profile employee of the airline and seasoned pilot, elected to take off before receiving the clearance from tower. His copilot never dared question him, afraid of his captain's possible anger at the question, leading to the catastrophic end well known as "The Tenerife Disaster"

Paternalistic:

Much like the Autocratic type, this manager tends to require or accept little or no input from the team in the decision making process. However, it differs by offering more attention to the individuals than the organization, focusing more on their well-being than the organizational goals or profit.

This type of management becomes more appropriate as teams or individuals evolve, gaining confidence and skills, and are able to work with less supervision. Although still keeping a very strict control on the goals and functioning of the teams, the focus moves from the end result to the individuals. This still leaves little room for initiative or innovative thinking, confining the team to a very much skill-related, goal-oriented work.

It is probably the most common type of cockpit management, introduced by the teaching of CRM during the early 80's. The Captain retains final responsibility and control over the complete team and goal settings, while promoting a better cohesion and communication between crew members. This in turn enhances safety but still does not allow the crew to fully perform their duties outside of maintaining predefined performance and safety standards.

Democratic:

Evolving from the paternalistic type, a democratic manager will not only focus on the team's individuals and their personal satisfaction, but also accepts input as part of the decision making process.

The information channels flow both ways, and bonds are created between managers and team members. By opening up communication, this type fosters a stronger sense of commitment from the individuals and the team, but it also slows down the decision making process.

It is easy to see how detrimental this could be when an emergency occurs or high-stress operations are in progress (congested airspace, take off/landing phases, etc), but it will provide a much better working environment on certain occasions. By allowing input from the team, planning becomes stronger as it assimilates multiple experience levels and knowledge basis – thus promoting a stronger "future" threat-mitigation. As the skill level and involvement of the team under such management tend to reach a higher level of professionalism, errors are less likely, also helping achieve an overall safe operation.

Laissez-Faire:

As a team reaches its full potential and the individuals' skills are at peak level, little or no supervision is required from the manager, whose focus turns back to the overall corporative or mission goals.

Each individual or team is given targets, but allowed space to take initiative on their own, pursue more evolved goals and, most importantly, innovate. Innovation will be the key to bringing a team from the "day-to-day grind" operational level to a truly successful, customer oriented service which will in turn change its focus from "goal/task-oriented" to "vision-driven". This form of management is best suited for highly skilled teams of professionals, who put more value on corporate success and vision than daily, low-skill tasks.

In the aviation environment, this management type will really shine with customer service and inter-corporate relations, but as the members find less fulfillment in the regular, "task-oriented" goals of the daily operations, a general sense of negligence or carelessness can settle in. This can cause a major threat to the safety of the operation, despite the high skill level of the team, as complacency takes place and seeps through the cracks of sloppy SOPs or checklist use, as well as an overconfidence and less attention to details.

It may seem like an easier alternative for a manager. But as a team carries on their duty with little to no supervision, the manager must sometimes revert back to a more autocratic style in order to maintain safety standards or attain targeted performance.

Chaotic

While the *Chaotic* management works well for creative companies such as Google, it has no place in a cockpit environment. Taking *Laissez-Faire* a step further, this enables a professional team to work with no supervision. Despite having a defined set of goals, they are given complete freedom as to how they achieve them and in what order.

Every time airlines merge, chaos ensues. It's inevitable. Pilots from two different operating philosophies are put together in the same cockpit, and required to operate an airline safely. Under this premise, it is very easy for one pilot to assume something was done, while the other pilot is completely unaware of any changes in duties.

Some captains may strike you as easy-going, but you quickly realize it's because they are going easy, without much care in the world about what everybody else is doing. They trust everyone so much to do their jobs, sometime including *their* job, that when things start heating up, their situational awareness is the first thing to go out the window.

If you recognize yourself or your coworker in this style, make sure to discuss with your team the proper or necessary changes needed to ensure a safe and efficient flight.

Which one is best?

There is truly no "better" management type. It is more important for a manager to be polyvalent and flexible, able to quickly adapt to the situation and use the appropriate type to deal with it. As airlines or other high-skill/high-stress operations evolve or hire new employees, there will always be challenges in focusing on the right aspect of the operation: Time? Performance? Passengers? Safety? – The common denominators will always be knowledge and training.

THE LEADER

So you can manage. But can you lead? Or maybe you can lead, but can you manage? Most people don't always realize that one is very different from the other. In fact, good managers rarely make good leaders, and good leaders rarely make good managers.[4] Why? Let's explore the issue.

While managers mostly focus on.. well, managing – situation, people, tasks, etc.. – a leader's role is to create a vision and get the team to adopt it, in order to move forward and grow. A Manager's role often lays in the "now", with task-driven skills. A Leader's role rather focuses in the "then", with people-driven skills.

You want a team to achieve a performance standard, or reach specific goals? A Manager will ensure the proper procedures are in place and that training standards will allow for peak performance. You want to engage people personally and drive them to commit to a vision, to generate forward momentum by tapping into creativity and innovation? Call upon a Leader!

Well you probably get the idea by now.

However, before more can be said about leadership, it's important to take a step back to understand the proverbial "big picture". Over the course of history, most tasks requiring leadership were physical, even all the way into the Industrial revolution and factory workers. The leadership model most appropriate at that time was called Leader-Follower, which was meant for optimized physical output from workers. This model had leaders make all the decisions and thinking, leaving the workers with only the tasks to follow orders and ask no questions.

But with the advent of technology, more and more of our workload has become cognitive. Yet the Leader-Follower model remains ingrained in our culture and proves less than optimal for our needs. As L. David Marquet (Captain, U.S. Navy, Retired) puts it: "Those who take orders usually run at half speed, underutilizing their imagination and initiative. While this doesn't matter much for rowing a trireme, it's everything for operating a nuclear-powered submarine."[5]

So how do we, as pilots, facilitate a more proactive and engaged participation from our team? The term is *empowerment*. It suggests a new leadership structure that would be called Leader-Leader, where we not only provide guidance, but also provide a means for our team to become engaged cognitively, take initiative and work proactively at fixing problems and finding solutions. It's important to note however that as control is delegated, technical skills must be strengthened and clear operational rules (SOPs) set out– both the roles of the manager.

In the book *Primal Leadership*, Daniel Goleman, who popularized the notion of emotional intelligence, describes six different styles of leadership. Not unlike managers, a good leader will know how to adapt and use the proper style[6] depending on the situation, all a variation of Leader-Follower and Leader-Leader structures. Let's explore them.

Visionary:

Simply put, a visionary leader focuses on the end goal. He paints a distant bull's-eye and then gets the team to aim at the same target, all the while moving closer and closer. He is the flag bearer in the battle, rallying the team, and charging forward towards their goal, ignoring the distractions and focusing on just moving forward. It is the team's responsibility to keep pace and follow.

This style is extremely valuable when a mission objective is compromised and a new goal must be set. Their uncanny ability to pull people in their wake make them powerful leaders when a change of direction is needed. But when the focus is solely on the objective, the chance for error is also moderate as the team does not always have time to properly plan or analyze potential threats. Individuals are forced to take calculated risks, but also have an open door to innovate and devise new or more efficient approaches to a goal or a challenge.

Coaching:

The coaching leader takes pride in the team and individuals. The focus shifts from simply reaching the end goal to allowing each team and individual to achieve their true potential in the process.

A coach helps individuals with initiative to develop and grow as professionals, showing them how to use their skills and link their personal or team's goals to the organization's goals. "Let me show you," he says, providing ideas, answers, and getting involved.

Care must be taken not to micromanage the team or individual's performance rather than teach them and allow for a natural learning curve. Allow them to grow, and experience the rewards of their hard work.

Affiliative:

The people person, the crowd pleaser. This leadership style is crucial when forming bonds between leader and employees, or trying to unify teams or individuals.

The affiliative leader's role is often a mediator's role. Mending relationships, creating trust, working personally and close with the individuals to create a corporate harmony, and thus allow progression towards a goal with minimal internal strife. They rely heavily on praise and positive comments.

If a leader is uncomfortable with offering constructive criticism or pointing out sub-par performance, they could jeopardize the goal and often the safety of the operation.

Democratic:

Just as the democratic manager above, this style of leadership taps into the collective knowledge-base of the team to bring about change or set goals, rather than on the single leadership of the visionary.

It will often prove useful when the leader does not have the knowledge or experience necessary to take a decision, opening the door to a deeper pool of wisdom from the people around. However, using this style often subjects a leader to two or more opinions or separate goals. A choice will have to be made. Compromise or cooperate?

A democratic leader will naturally have an affiliative character. Compromise will seem like the better option as it reduces the interpersonal friction between differing opinions or teams. However, it also undermines the leader's power and thus reduces greatly the success of the team, rendering only mediocre results. Cooperation requires more work especially on the interpersonal level, but will yield far better results. Ask yourself: Would you EVER compromise on safety?

Democracy can also be detrimental, even downright dangerous, when urgent situations arise. In an airplane environment, democracy needs to take the back seat when decisions need to be made rapidly in order to ensure the safety of the people on board. The next kind of leader bears that role much more suitably.

Pacesetting:

This leader is a performance freak. Everything needs to be done better, faster, and to the highest standards. Always asking more of themselves and their team members, the pacesetters drive their team relentlessly towards their goal, while never allowing a drop in performance.

Pilots are no strangers to high-stress environments, where performance is critical and the demand can remain high for an extended period of time. However, the human body and mind are not designed to sustain such a pace for ever, and a continuous demand can eventually bring rapid decrease in performance. Fatigue settles in opening the door to errors, impairing the judgment of potential threats.

Leaders must learn when to use this style and more importantly how long before their team collapses. In emergency situations it will be required and necessary, but during routine operations a different style would be appropriate.

Commanding:

An even harsher version of the pacesetting leader, the commander uses the military style of leadership. This style is used less often as it provides very limited success. Criticism takes the place of praise, and harsh commands replace coaching and counseling. "Do as I say, and do it NOW!"

It is easy to see how a crew facing a life threatening situation could (and probably should) quickly revert back to this style. Trust your crew's training and direct commands in order to take full advantage of it. No questions asked, only an intricate trust between crew and leader, that one knows what he's asking for, and the other knows what he's doing. Only then can this style truly shine.

Otherwise it is generally recommended to avoid commanding your teams around as it completely destroys any ability they have to innovate and grow as professionals.

What leader are you?

Chances are, you probably saw one of these and said "AH HA! there! I knew I could be a leader!" That's great! However, as previously mentioned with the managers, you probably need to see this more as a swiveling chair with 6 desks around it. As a leader, you will occupy the chair, but different teams, goals or situations will often require you to use a different desk to better answer to the needs. Are you up for it?

ARE YOU A LEADER, OR A MANAGER?

The reality of it is, however, that in an airline or team-driven environment, certain people will be required to wear both hats. But how do you decide which hat to wear? When does your team look up to you as a leader or a manager? Here is my conclusion to the dilemma:

> *"A cockpit needs a Manager. An airplane needs a Leader."*
> *– Author, The Pilot Factor*

Manage your cockpit. Use SOP and CRM to ensure the procedures in place are followed in order to face every flight phase as predicated and minimize risk of errors, as well as mitigate any threat that might arise. Training+Performance=Safety, and it's the manager's role to always promote this very equation.

Lead your crew. More often than not in any commercial operation, there is more than just two pilots involved in the flight. You may have cabin crew (or paramedics even!) in the back, and they have their own managers. The aircraft can only have one leader however, and this responsibility befalls the Captain. Set the tone for the flight, create an atmosphere of commitment towards the client and passion for the brand, and in moments of crisis, boldly lead your crew towards success.

> *"You cannot manage men into battle. You Manage things. You Lead men."*
> *-Admiral U.S. Navy (Ret'd) Grace Hopper*

Conclusion

Here is a little recap I found very useful. I realize that often times, the captain's job can be quite demanding. But more often than not, First Officers are tasked with the impossible job of being virtual chameleons. As an FO, you will be required to mold your work pace and expectations to every different captain's management or leadership style. I hope this will also help you, and in some way, increase your ability to support your captain in his or her duties.

Management	Leadership
To Produce Order	To Produce Change
To Achieve Consistency	To Achieve a Vision
Planning	Setting the Direction
Coping with Complexity	Coping with Change
Independent Functions	Interdependent Functions
Positive Control	Motivating
Other Directed	Self-Directed
Reactive	Proactive

(The Center for Organizational and Professional Excellence)

REVIEW QUESTIONS

1. Lead from the _____, Manage from the _____

2. What Management Style do you naturally fall back to?

3. What Leadership Style do you naturally fall back to?

4. A chief pilot needs to create new operating procedures to promote a heightened safety culture. Is this part of his Leadership or Management role?

5. A First Officer witnesses a potentially dangerous situation. Can or should (s)he assume a Leadership role and convince others in the crew to "do things right"?

TEAM COHESION

Stress, Skills, Training. Play your strengths and know your limits!

The cockpit came to a standstill for a few moments. As the sound of the engine spooling down subsided, only the faint scratching of my pen racing along the empty lines of the daily flight documents could be heard. Another successful flight! Well, not quite...

Breaking the short silence, my captain's voice almost startles me more than his frantic announcement, "We have a FIRE!" (Bear in mind this is paraphrased to save your eyes from the more... colorful wording actually used). I look up to the engine cowling of our PC12, but nothing seems out of the ordinary there. Where's the fire?

I shift my eyes to the exhaust pipe on my side of the nose, and I am greeted by flames shooting past me, all the way to the door – bright and furious. Both of us go from standstill to full speed. In a split second we are both engaged in a battle against time, working as a team to vanquish this fire-breathing dragon that our airplane had just turned into.

The first words spoken are, "we need to evacuate!" But is that the safest thing to do? With flames blocking our natural egress through the main door, and with line crew personnel barely feet away from us on the ramp, a different plan is quickly devised. Our brains race against time, quickly re-evaluating the situation. A new plan is proposed. "How about running the engine without injecting fuel, to snuff out the flames and cool it down?"

These crucial seconds of discussion were, in my opinion, the very heart of CRM. Both crew members offered solutions, evaluated and together acted on the best plan of action. The engine was later pronounced a total loss, but we protected the immediate safety of all occupants onboard the airplane as well as the well-being of the adjacent line personnel, while containing and neutralizing the threat.

This event led to what was for me a defining landmark in my aviation career. The ensuing investigation into what could have been, I will admit, a much better managed incident, taught me that no matter how seasoned a pilot, there is always need to constantly strive to learn, improve, challenge and better one-self both skill-wise and knowledge-wise. The learning process will teach you more about yourself than you ever imagined, and allow you to become an inherent part of your team's success.

After 8 hours of uneventful flying, completing multi-legs missions in clear-sky weather, the job can hardly be called stressful. Yet when 6 feet long flames stream past you barely a foot away, suddenly your day just took a pretty stressful turn. How do you lead and manage your team in order to achieve success, when unforeseen and highly demanding and stressful events occur?

Technical training will provide you with the basic tools and understanding to manage the airplane. But to lead your team effectively, you need to know its strengths and weaknesses. By understanding your team, operational performance will come easier, and interpersonal team cohesion will become second nature.

In retrospect, I realized that although the situation ended up being contained and managed to a safe end through good CRM, it wasn't *perfect* CRM. Our recollection of the events while participating in the investigation revealed how much the stress and present threat of fire had affected our efficiency.

Did we clearly communicate everything we were doing or seeing? Did we action the proper checklists? Did we explain the situation concisely to our paramedics to ensure their safe cooperation?

Although we both had the same goal – protect the people and neutralize the threat – we failed in some respect to work seamlessly together and achieve it in a much more effective way because of miscommunications and divergent priorities.

Was it the **stress**? Was our **decision making** a factor? Was it the lack of **training or skills**? Or was it that we had not **clearly set targets** as a crew, even from the beginning of the day?

STRESS

People are subjected to stress in many ways. It can have a physical impact as well as an emotional factor. It has also been argued that it is a matter of perception, measured and quantified cognitively by the brain.

Perceived Stress

The appraisal process can be crucial to understanding and responding to a stressful event. Understand how your brain works and interacts with a situation, and you will be much better equipped to manage any amount of stress.

Outside of the immediate situation which the brain is perceiving as stressful, other important factors influence judgment or performance through stress. The expectations you have of your environment, if altered, are common perceived stressors.

The consequences you believe an outcome may produce will also affect your decision making. "Will I reduce the potential threat better by following my instinct or by following the checklist first?"

Additional stressors of note are "emotion, insight, perceived expectations of peers, supervisors or family, confidence in one's capability to deal with a situation, and perceived general workload." [1]

The psychologist Lazarus [2] described perceived stress as a two-part cognitive process. He called them the *Primary* and *Secondary Appraisal.* The names may be misleading, as the brain does not do the Primary THEN the Secondary, but rather constantly underline the cognitive process of the former with the later.

Primary Appraisal:

It is important to understand that both personal and environmental/circumstantial factors (time constraints, skill level required, etc.) both influence the "primary appraisal", which in turns affects the different potential solutions. In short, this "first impression" of the situation will tell you how "stressful" the problem is, and how to prioritize and allocate resources to fix it.

Let's go back to the original story behind this chapter.

As we went from a no-stress to a high-stress situation, both naturally started evaluating the circumstances. A visible fire and immediate danger to the airplane as well as the line personnel outside the aircraft dictated a rapid response and full commitment from both crew members.

We had a choice: Use cockpit resources (checklist, system knowledge, etc.) to contain the fire, or evacuate the aircraft to secure personnel outside? Experience and training both played a crucial role in the decision making process.

In our case, we decided to contain the fire from within. After appraising the situation – engine temperature spike, visible flames, and personnel at risk outside. My brain prioritized and I acted accordingly to achieve these three safety targets:

- **Manage the problem**. Running checklists and completing necessary steps to diffuse the potential danger of the situation, removing the fire threat;

- **Manage myself**. Being aware of fear, confusion, and survival instinct to ensure proper communication between the flight crew and cabin crew

- **Manage others**. Prevent panic – which would most likely produce injuries if somebody attempted to act on their own out of fear. Emotions – meaning "Energy in Motion" – can have a serious impact on the outcome of a situation. Having the ability to direct their "energy" the right way is a crucial skill set every team member must master. Giving a simple task to a panicked crewmember can help provide guidance and manage their stress by focusing their attention on something else.

More often than not, in high-stress situations, we face those challenges. Focusing on ONLY the problem can create tunnel vision and cause the crew to overlook the need for proper communication with other parties or even secondary problems. But only focusing on the negative emotions and dealing with people instead of the problem can cause aggravation of the original situation, increasing the stress level exponentially – especially if proper communication has failed in the meantime and fear or panic starts taking hold.

Secondary appraisal

As you appraise the situation and the stress (danger potential or priority level) it will also create an inventory of the things you need, have or lack to respond properly to it: Time? Skill level? Experience? Man power? This is referred to as the "Secondary Appraisal".

As it evaluates the resources, the brain then alters the primary appraisal to readjust priorities, juggling problem and emotions to achieve the balance required to deal properly with an ever evolving scenario.

In short, as the secondary appraisal determines whether resources become more or less available, the brain basically dials the perceived stress level down or up accordingly through primary appraisal.

Adapt

High stress and skill-demanding professions mean problem solving and conflict resolution are a daily part of our jobs. Your ability to cognitively assess a situation correctly is crucial and training plays a huge part in this. The bigger challenge is adapting to an escalating situation successfully. Not only that, there are times where you will need to adapt your leadership style as circumstances change.

You may be a democratic leader for example, who likes to take in input from the team and keep everybody happy. But when an emergency arises, asking for everyone's opinion is usually not the best route to successfully resolving it. Your responsibility will dictate that you change your leadership style into a more commanding tone and take direct control of the situation.

You've probably heard of that principle many times in the course of your career or training: Problem and Conflict Resolution. Without going into details, the resolution means that the threat is gone and/or the target has been achieved. But resolution requires the individual/team to examine the effectiveness of the problem solving or stress coping; if it is not having the desired effect, a different strategy will need to be implemented.

A flexible mind and adaptable personality are key tools to any individual or team.

Examine the Situation. Understand the needs and constraints. Manage (and if need be, change) your priorities. Review the situation – if it is not resolved, adapt your approach to create a more efficient response to the threat.

TOOLS OF THE TRADE: EXPERIENCE, SKILLS AND TRAINING

A successful businessman who, during an interview, was asked the secret to his success.

"Good decisions" he says, without hesitation.

The interviewer, not skipping a beat, asks, "How did you learn to make good decisions?"

The man answered, "Bad Decisions."

As Oscar Wilde stated: "Experience is simply the name we give our mistakes". These few words illustrate a fundamental truth: No matter how much knowledge you acquire through training, successful critical thinking is a combination of training and experience. An experienced team has intuition, better understanding of the mechanics – both human and technical – and can adapt much easier. In the face of threat, experience provides a much broader ability to react swiftly and attain safety quickly. Experience also provides a much finer filter for possible errors, eliminating threats even before they become a potential danger.

Training

> *"We do not rise to the level of our expectations. We fall to the level of our training" -Unknown source.*

Training is the first line of defense against potential errors and eventual threats which may arise. We train to perform to certain standards, but we also train to respond to certain events. Checklists, manuals, and drills mold our minds and condition us to a standard skill level. In the case of training, however, testing standards do not provide a true demonstration of one's ability to handle stress in the face of a threat, but rather the ability to play a pre-determined script at a pre-required skill level. It is up to the airline/employer to enhance the training with interpersonal and leadership development.

Training is essential and provides the foundation needed to build skills and experience upon. But training alone does not provide the tools for successful threat and error management in the work environment – rather it allows one to basically function as part of a team in a supporting function.

Students or inexperienced pilots can often perceive a situation as more threatening, more stressful than it actually is. Because of their lack of confidence in their skill or experience level, their decision making ability is often self-limited. Instead, it is important that they take a mental step back and cognitively evaluate the problem.

The *Perceive, Process, Perform* (**3P**) model offers a very simple yet practical and systematic decision making approach that can be used at any time and by any pilot – student or experienced. The FAA[3] describes it as:

- Perceive the given set of circumstances for a flight

- Process by evaluating their impact on flight safety

- Perform by implementing the best course of action.

Sometimes, even an experienced crew will come across a situation for which they have not been trained or have no experience with. How do *they* deal with those?

One blustery winter night, my air ambulance team was dispatched to pick up a patient from a nearby community. Heavy snow squalls were forecasted at our destination, but it was nothing unusual for this time of the year, so we launched without much of a second thought.

Closing on our destination, I contacted the tower for an update on the weather. "The reported visibility is 2 statute miles. Last airplane reported very reduced visibility on touch-down." Discussing this last update with the captain, we figured that if we had enough visibility to *land* the airplane, we should certainly be able to *taxi* it in. Makes sense, no?

Having both agreed to proceed with the approach, I called out the regular checklists and approach items as the captain masterfully flew the airplane through what can only be described as a *blizzard.* Rough winds, windshear, snow and night time all demanded his sharpest skills. But nothing prepared us for what happened after our wheels touched pavement.

As the nose wheel lowered onto the runway, the visibility went from *little* to *none.* We could barely see the next set of runway lights! Needless to say we were very grateful for our advanced avionics, which had automatically brought up the airport's diagram on one of our big LCD screens. While I stared at the map to provide guidance, the skipper slowly turned the aircraft around on the runway and headed for the nearest exit.

Lacking the ability to see very far, however, the captain glimpsed what *seemed* to be the entrance to the taxiway, and carefully headed towards it. But something wasn't right. With my eyes going back-and-forth between outside and the moving map display, it looked as if we were headed not for the entrance, but straight to the *edge* of the taxiway!

I warned the captain, who immediately stopped. But it was too late. We had stopped with our front wheel barely inches from the snow bank. With no room to spare and a strong wind working against us, there was no way for us to safely turn away from the edge and back onto the taxiway. Time was now against us, as we were informed by the tower that the land ambulance crew had just arrived with our patient.

At that moment, I learned an incredible lesson. Instead of going into panic mode or trying to make a rushed decision, the captain simply shut down the engine. I still wasn't too sure of exactly *why* he had rendered us completely powerless in the middle of all this! But his decision had, I believe, a *profound* impact on the positive safety of our expedition.

Turning to me, he explained his plan, "Let's take a moment, and figure out our options. I want to make sure and take the time to plan our way out without rushing or risking any oversights."

This effectively led to all four of us (both paramedics and pilots) to jump outside into the blizzard. Now laughing at this bizarre blizzard situation, we worked as a team to push the airplane back far enough to allow for a safe turn towards the paved taxiway. Using all the tools possible, we safely proceeded to our ambulance rendezvous point.

The captain took one final step to ensure mental *and* equipment readiness before heading back into the blizzard once more. Deliberately taking more time than usual, we conducted a thorough walk around and briefing. With all stress gone, our team was now ready for its next journey.

This **analytical decision model** was useful to us and probably saved us a lot more trouble down the road. Requiring a deliberate and lengthier approach, it is often a very powerful method when faced with complex situation and no experience or readily available tools. It is known as the **DECIDE**[3] model.

DECIDE MODEL
Detect – Detect the problem **Estimate** – Estimate the need for counter-measures or react to the change **Choose** – Choose a safe outcome **Identify** – Identify the actions which will successfully control the change **Do** – Implement the chosen actions **Evaluate** – Evaluate the effect of action in countering the change and progress of the flight

Training will often enable you to correctly evaluate the variables of the *DECIDE* model:

- Risk or hazard

- Potential outcomes (What is desired? SOP, COM, Safety?)

- Capabilities of pilot (Knowledge, comfort level, etc.)

- Aircraft capabilities (AFM limitations, checklist, etc.)

- Outside factors (weather, time constraints, etc.)

But, when Training does not answer the need for proficient operations and threat management, what comes next? What tools will allow us to successfully and safely deal with a stressful or hazardous situation?

Skill

Skill level is a factor of training quality. To achieve team cohesion in a high-skill, high-stress job, the leader/manager must ensure his team members demonstrate and maintain the required level of standards they honed during training. Only once every team member has demonstrated satisfactory skill level can desired safety and performance be expected.

Skill development however does not stop at training standards. An individual or team should always strive to enhance their performance by acquiring new skills, and constantly train to better their skill level. It is hard to do so without a supporting structure or system within the company itself, and so it befalls the leaders to set the proper vision and pace – allowing their team room to grow and learn.

Experience

Whether you are a student pilot or a seasoned commercial pilot, you will by now have made a lot of decisions. Decisions are what define our world. Decisions are what we get paid for. Any high-stress job is based on decision making – that's why it is so stressful. Our brain is constantly reviewing information, analyzing, turning images upside down and trying to discover the hidden angle.

Albert Einstein once said, "The only source of knowledge is Experience." The cognitive process of analyzing, storing and then retrieving past events and outcomes to help with a current problem is what we call experience. Whether you are conscious of it or not, your past experience always affects your reasoning on new problems. You learn what worked well, what required lots of work. The failures, the successes, all turning points in your personal growth, affecting your team's performance directly.

It is not always realistic to expect the luxury of time when making critical decisions. In the face of an emergency, a pilot or crew will often call upon their previous experiences to help rapidly analyze and respond to the threat. Taking too much time to weigh all the options can even sometimes be detrimental to a safe outcome if time is of the essence.

Research into people's decision-making patterns has demonstrated that when pressed for time, experts (experienced and skilled people) faced with task and uncertain variables will first try to evaluate it against any other similar experience they may have. Instead of weighing every option, they look for the quickest safe way out. While it may not be the *best* solution, it will still yield positive results.

Facing the flames coming out of our exhaust in my opening story, time was very limited due to the extreme temperatures in the engine and the immediate danger of the fire. There was no checklist for our particular event. Instead, my brain mentally compared what knowledge I had formed training against stories or situations which could relate, and extrapolated the fastest viable solution to eliminate the presence of flames outside of the engine's controlled environment.

The terms **naturalistic** and **automatic decision-making**[3] are used to describe this process. It hinges on the recognition of patterns and consistencies that simplify options in complex situations. By using experience and knowledge together, a pilot or team can now act quickly by creatively adapting to the situation.

Experience comes with benefits... and pitfalls. One of the benefits is the proportionate reduction of stress when facing various threats. Although not all events are the same, many bear similarities. An experienced team member is able to glean from past problems and resolutions to put together an answer for a specific occurrence. By extrapolating the results of past outcomes and resources requirements, the brain's cognitive process recognizes a pattern and reduces the level of stress through familiarity. An emergency or non-standard event may seem very stressful the first time, but the second or third time it becomes easier and easier to resolve the situation and it appears much less dire than the first impression.

However, over time, experience can become conducive to complacency. The false feeling of security and the reduced attention to details reopens the door wide open to operational errors, which in turn can pose additional internal threats to the safety or positive conclusion of a targeted goal.

An experienced team or individual can now start to shift their focus from threat resolution to threat avoidance. Experience, along with high skill levels, allows for a low cognitive demand during regular operations, even for seemingly "stressful" executions (take off, landing, etc.) A complacent team will settle down in a routine and keep their focus on "the big picture". Complacency must be broken to allow the focus to shift from big to small, now bringing the team's attention to the details surrounding the operations.

> *"Excellence is not a skill. It is an attitude."* -Ralph Marston

To achieve excellence in performance and safety, the mold of routine must be broken. No – I am not crazy. Routine is good, but complacency prevents creativity and innovation. Complacency enables errors to creep in, and stops a "good" team from being "amazing".

SET YOUR EXPECTATIONS

When working with experienced individuals, teach them to break the mold and think critically, creatively, and outside the box of routine. When they achieve their goals, they will then push on to achieve excellence.

As the team **Leader**, or Captain, it is primordial for you to set the tone from the first encounter with your team members at the beginning of a work day or session. Lay out your vision of the day in a concise way, what you expect to achieve, and make sure everybody is clear on their roles and responsibilities. When a problem arises, the chain of command then is there to help but less crucial as team members can start taking initiative within their own roles and work together towards a resolution rather than always turn to the leader.

As a team **Manager**, or Captain, it is your job to set a clear standard of skill requirement and operational standards. These requirements may vary from day to day depending on external circumstances, becoming more or less demanding depending on the expected "stress" level that will be imposed, but always set to at least a safe, quantifiable level – your SOPs and COM being the very basic minimum requirements.

With clear standards and expectations set, the team becomes a lot more efficient at reaching safety targets and operational goals. Less supervision is required, leaving more time and resources to deal with the smaller details, passengers' needs or operational changes that may arise during the day. Communication becomes clearer with less information needing to be exchanged, reducing the risk for error. Threats are more easily assessed based on a well-defined set of rules, eventually leading to the goal of every professional team. A seamless operation of excellence and safety. Remove the mold, and open the door to innovation.

> *"One of the things that limits our learning is our belief that we already know something" - Captain (U.S. Navy, Ret'd) L.David Marquet*

REVIEW QUESTIONS

1. What tends to elevate your stress level? People? Situations?

2. Now that you know Stress is perceptual, can you recall a situation where better training or experience might have changed the level of perceived   stress?

3. Describe in your own words the 3 "P"s of decision making

Perceive:

Process:

Perform:

4. Are you more of an Analytical or Naturalistic decision maker?

5. Describe a time when your decision making style has been an asset or liability to resolving a situation?

TEAM REVIEW

The secrets and benefits of debriefing

Every flight student has those painfully vivid memories of certain points in time during their training. They cringe when retelling the story of their first "wheelbarrow" landing, or smile proudly at the recollection of a rather well-executed full instrument approach. To me, that moment in time was not defined by an event – but rather by a person.

Before I continue with the story, however, I must profess that I had some of the best, most knowledgeable and patient flight instructors a student could ask for. But I must also confess that I am not always the smartest. My motto "Practice doesn't make perfect, Perfect practice makes perfect" is a true telling of my performance. On one particular day, having jumped in the flight school's twin engine PA31-Navajo, my instructor and I set out to, well, practice. The IFR training curriculum required many practiced holding patterns, course navigation and instrument approaches. Nevertheless, I was ecstatic. Having just transitioned form the single engine trainers to this powerful little twin engine, I felt like I was on top of the world.

Soaring into the sky with a resounding RRROOARR, the rhythmic beat of our two turbocharged engines almost set the pace as we settled into the training routine. Intercept a course. Hold at a fix. Prepare for the approach. Having obtained the most recent weather from the airport automated reporting, the prognostic looked good. A solid overcast layer over the airport offered us a chance to practice real instrument flying while still giving us a safe margin for training. As we started our decent my heart began to beat a little faster. The excitement, coupled with the stress of the learning curve, were making me feel more alive than ever. Then suddenly...

"WHAT are you doing?" the voice of my instructor snapped me out of my reverie. "What comes next? Always stay ahead of the airplane! You should be lowering the landing gear by now!" As he continued on my spirit sank to the ground. I WAS about to lower the landing gear, couldn't he have given me one more second? As we went down the approach and completed the landing, the instructor's voice continued to ring as he debriefed me on my performance at the same time as everything else was happening. Needless to say that my performance found itself as low as my spirits. I could not bring myself to concentrate on the exercises at hand while my senses and wits were dulled by the continuing tirade of comments and "pointers". Feeling emotionally and mentally drained, I let out a sigh of relief when the flight eventually came to an end.

Walking back to the instructor's office, I replayed the events in my head. In truth, it had not been a very successful flight training-wise. Had I been given the chance to rectify the situation with a simple pointer or reminder, while debriefing the problems afterwards, I would have remembered much more from that flight than just my instructor's voice in my headset. Instead, well, there's the story you just read. From then on, I vowed to myself to never jeopardize the safety or learning potential of a flight by trying to debrief a coworker (Captain, FO or even cabin crew) until the time was right and everybody had a chance to talk with a level head.

So this brings me to one of the final chapters of this study. Did you encounter a threat during the flight which you had to manage? Did a crew member make an error which could or did jeopardize the safety of the flight? Nevertheless, a *timely* and *structured* debriefing is crucial to gaining experience from the event and moving forward to a better performance and safety the next time. As I mentioned in the story, timely certainly does not mean while the event is occurring. So let's talk about debriefing.

HISTORY AND EVOLUTION

During WWII, US Army's Chief Historian – Brigadier General Marshall – performed the first historical group debriefing.[1] As soldiers recounted events of combat, feelings and how it impacted their decisions, some surprising and unexpected findings were made.

Some psychological benefits were found, bringing about a deeper interest into the matter. However, it wasn't until the 80s that actual research was carried out more thoroughly. In 1983, a psychologist named Mitchell who worked with hospital emergency services personnel developed a method of debriefing called Critical Incident Stress Debriefing (CISD), using Marshall's work as a foundation[2]. There were of course attempts at debriefing before then, but their records were dubious and left a lot of questions as to their content and effectiveness.

A few years later, Dyregrov, the director of the Norwegian Center of Crisis Psychology, further modified Mitchell's method to create a slightly more complex system[3]. Finally, it wasn't until the Golf War that Frank Parkinson, a US Army Chaplain, developed his own three-stage model after working with soldiers coming out of the war. His own variation of this model called "3 F"[4] has become a modern benchmark. One last major model called "Emotional Decompression Model" geared towards post-traumatic stress syndrome was later created. However, this model does not relate to our study's needs.

WHY IS DEBRIEFING IMPORTANT?

"Experience is something you don't get until just after you need it." – *Steven Wright.*

During the flurry of development and research on the subject in the 80s, Lederman coined a very important term: Cognitive Assimilation of Experience.[5] In three words, he summarized the absolute necessity and reason of debriefing. *Experience.*

In order to gain knowledge and skills – experience – from past events, we have to be able to make sense of them. We have to learn new ways of seeing, perceiving, & making sense of experience. Debriefing gives us a powerful tool to structure the process. As individuals or a group, we can then pull out the crucial information that will allow us to learn from past experiences.

"What went wrong?" is a powerful learning tool, but it is also a reactionary one. It gives us great hindsight on the Errors and Undesired States which jeopardized the flight. Only through this process however, can we then reduce the potential error factor, thus further enhancing the safety and effectiveness of future operations.

A DEBRIEFING'S COMPONENTS

There are necessary skills to a successful debrief. Mastering them is not easy and dedicated training is usually *de rigueur*. However, Debriefing is an important tool to understand and have. Any team leader or member should understand its basics steps, needs, and benefits.

So to better understand this, we need to analyze and understand the following key elements:

Communication
First and foremost, communication is key. Trust and respect between the crew are the catalysts to proper dialog. Understanding the variations of communications style and how we each express ourselves differently will allow a frustration-free debriefing, allowing the crew to instead concentrate on the issues being discussed.

Time matters
When to engage into debriefing is the reason that prompted this chapter in the first place. Although this is a controversial factor, the importance of timing cannot be stressed enough. *When* to select the right time for a discussion has been a big part of the research on Debriefing. Dyregrov divided his research in communication into two parts[6].

- **Timing:** The ability to know *when* to engage into debriefing is usually a factor of experience. Trial and error will be your best friends, but some basics remain. Avoid at all cost to start the process *during* the event. It will dramatically reduce the proficiency level and proportionally increase the risk for errors and problems while your crew is subjected to multiple cognitive processes at the same time. Make mental or written notes and if needed take corrective measures to ensure safe or efficient operations, but keep the debriefing for after.

Time proximity to the event will often be dictated by external factors: A long flight, different priorities upon mission completion, availability of crew, etc. Allowing time between the event and the debrief allows "hind-sight" to help clarify things before discussing them, but waiting too long can hinder the correct recollection of important details.

- **Length:** Once engaged in debriefing, make sure to moderate it to avoid unnecessary lengthy debates and keep it focused on the objectives or problems at hand. Silence can be a powerful tool as well, promoting self-questioning introspection. This in turn promotes more open and honest discussion.

Emotion

Events that require debriefing usually contain a certain element of stress. Stress is often a synonym to emotions as part of the decision making cognitive process. This then leads to the understanding of emotional intelligence, and the role it plays. Finally we land back at the beginning of our journey, where we learned about *TEAM Assessment*. Every part of the pilot factor is intrinsically connected, as emotions, communications and experience play a symbiotic role in a successful and safe operation or mission.

Structure

According to the history of debriefing, there are four major models – Mitchell/Dyregrov/Three-Stage/Emotional Decompression. All have been created based on psychological training and backgrounds, but their uses vary depending on the context.

For use in a team/crew environment, I recommend Parkinson's "3 F". This Three-Stage method provides structure for debriefing process with 3 segments in question format:

The Facts

- What was happening *before* the incident

- What happened *during* the incident

- What happened *after* the incident

The Feelings

- Sensory impressions (sight, sound, smell, touch, taste)

- Emotions – what feelings and emotions were generated?

- Reactions – How did you react then? How does that make you feel now? Anything positive?

The Future

- Normalization – Understand that to err is human, analyze the human factor in the event

- What can we **learn** going forward? Extrapolate into **experience** that can be shared and taught, or **policies** that can be implemented

- Provide support (personal, organizational, etc.) if needed

CONCLUSION

Debriefing enables and enhances *experience*. It allows us to cognitively process information and learn from an event or a series of events. At the end of the day, the debriefing you carry out will be the turning point for your team. You will either leave having gained knowledge and skill, or you will end with a bitter taste in your mouth. The following three tips will ensure you stay on the right track when releasing your team after a debrief.

Accentuate the *positive*. Underestimating the power of positive thinking will quickly undermine all your efforts to create an atmosphere of learning. Never leave your team hanging on a negative note after a debrief. It *will* be the only thing they remember. Many experiences can be perceived as negative especially in a high-stress and performance-based environment. It is, however, the responsibility of the leader to ensure that the team or individuals concludes the experience on a positive note to enhance the value and quality of the lessons to be learned.

Higher Order Thinking. Lessons can be learned only if they can be understood. The saying, "Hindsight is 20/20," offers great value. As you conclude your debrief, keep the objectives of your team in sigh: Safety and Performance. Use these objectives as reference to extract as much learning material as possible when bench-marked against them.

Experience Counts: Don't stop there. The end of a briefing is only the beginning of a much broader process: teaching and training. Use all the resources available to propagate this new experience and allow other teams or individuals to learn from it while they train and prepare for their own work. This is the very heart of programs like SMS (Safety Management System), which airlines, hospitals and other skill-demanding or inherently dangerous/stressful environment need to implement or have implemented to ensure the successful and safe operation of their business.

Training+Performance=Safety. Training is acquired through the process of sharing knowledge through a structured process and with respect to the emotions involved.

Remember:

People will forget what you did.

People will forget what you said.

But people will never forget what you made them feel.

So Debrief, Learn, and Share!

REVIEW QUESTIONS

1. Describe a time where a debriefing could have been helpful but was carried out at a bad time, or with the focus on the wrong items?

2. Describe in your own words the 3 "F"s of debriefing

Facts:

Feelings:

Future:

3. How can lessons learned from debriefings be used to help enhance the day-to-day operations?

4. Debriefs are crucial. What about briefings? How can they help? If debriefs tackle the "Errors & Undesired States" would Briefings be a good countermeasure to "Threats"?

TEAM SUCCESS

The Super-Hero Syndrome

> **Loki:** What have I to fear?
> **Tony Stark:** The Avengers. It's what we call ourselves. Sorta like a team. Earth's Mightiest Heroes type thing.
> **Loki:** Yes. I've met them
> **Tony Stark:** Yeah, takes us a while to get any traction I'll give you that one. But let's do a head count here. Your brother, the demigod. A super soldier, living legend who kinda lives up to the legend. A man with breathtaking anger management issues.
>   - *Marvel,* The Avengers

I've always been an Avengers fan. Not only for their incredible deeds and awesome powers –not to mention killer looks – but also for their ability to work together despite their most unique disparity and clash of personalities and backgrounds.

I mean think of it: Men and women, aliens, demi-gods, and, well, Tony Stark, all coming together and working together as an (almost) cohesive team to achieve their goals. It amazes me every time. The very first time I watched the movie in the theater, it struck me how close the resemblance can be to many flight crews and other highly-skilled teams: Immense egos (Stark) colliding with brute force characters (Hulk, SMASH!), trying to work with powerful yet somewhat antiquated (Captain America) thinkers, while a strong female figure (Black Widow) uses her more or less charming ways to also pull her weight. Wow.

Being superheroes didn't help them be better people, and only after much internal struggle did they eventually come together as a TEAM. Then and only then were they able to prevail and achieve their goal.

Rings a bell? I thought it would. We all have come across those types in our careers. The Egomaniac, the old-fashioned thinker... I could make a list. The truth is, I could probably name myself in that list somewhere. Can you?

What have your experiences been when facing such a character? Most of the time a confrontation with a superhero leaves bruises and leads to much frustration, headaches and problems. Take even our beloved Captain Kirk. Bold and brave leader as he was, he was also called "a tin-plated overbearing, swaggering dictator with delusions of godhood".

History tells us of an event where a pilot turned mass-killer because he refused to let go of his super-ego.

It was the day without an end. Already tired from hours of flying, his airplane was now grounded at a small airport with many others. Their arrival airport had been shut down temporarily so all inbound flights had had to divert. To make matters worse, the weather was now deteriorating rapidly into a dense fog. Passengers were hungry, and people wanted answers. As the most senior pilot at his airline, he couldn't lose face. He *wouldn't* lose face. His airplane would get airborne soon again, no matter the cost.

"At least, I'll be the first to leave," he thought. Having parked his airplane nearest to the runway, he'd ensured that nobody would get to depart before he did. Although he wasn't first in line to get fuel, he had blocked the way to the way for any other aircrafts with his massive 747.

Finally! With his destination airport reopened and the airplane's fuel tanks full once more, he was more than ready to leave. Back in the cockpit with his first officer, they prepared for departure. Running through the checklists as fast as they could, communication was sparse for time's sake.

Rushing to backtrack the runway, he deliberately kept the aircraft's communications to a minimum with the control tower. It was frustrating. They'd never dealt with such heavy traffic before, and it was hard to understand them through their broken English accent anyway. If only this fog wasn't so dense...

Suddenly, his well-laid plan was compromised. Another Jumbo-Jet was instructed to taxi behind them on the same runway. His chance of getting out before the weather got even worse was now jeopardized. But he would not get stuck behind. Not him. His duty was to get the flight to destination, and he would see to that.

As they reached the end of the runway and started turning around to align for take-off, the controllers radioed in a new clearance. "Line up and wait, Pan-Am 747 exiting runway ahead". The KLM captain, Jacob Veldhuyzen van Zanten, saw it as his opportunity to get ahead, an open door to the skies. He didn't need anybody's consent or approval. He was master and commander of this airplane.

Did his officer try to stop him? Or did the captain's "leadership" eradicate any sign of resistance from the crew?

The fog was so dense they could not see very far down the runway. But the other aircraft would be out of the way in time. Wouldn't they? The sound of his questioning conscience was soon drowned by the roar of 200,000lbs of thrust coming alive. They moved slowly at first. Then faster, and faster, they accelerated down the runway blindly.

Seconds later, the two colossal 747s collided. The Pan-Am aircraft was still on the runway, looking for their exit in the very low visibility.

With one final stroke to his ego, Captain van Zanten had become the most infamous captain in the history of civil aviation, sealing the fate of 583 people[1].

Where does that leave us? You and I work in a highly competitive industry, where your success is measured by your abilities and skills – your powers. We are all superheroes in our minds, comparing each other continuously and gauging each other's powers and accomplishments. But often times we are called to work together, unite as a team to achieve a bigger goal, complete a bigger mission, while keeping collateral damage at a record low if possible.

Every team is different, and individuals will bring in their strengths and weaknesses. So only by working together can you reach your team's (and individual) full potential, complete efficiency, and eliminate the threats and errors that may arise. With the lives of people in hand every day you work, or higher stakes than some could even imagine possible, you are truly superheroes every time you deliver them safely at destination or reach your target goal, whatever it may be.

During these last chapters, we have covered all the super powers you will need to allow you to:

1. Understand your team (Assessment, Communication)

2. Work with your team (Training, Awareness, Decision Making)

3. Lead your team (Leadership, Cohesion, Debriefing)

As a team, you will need to apply these principles every day. This will be the challenge, as you face your greatest enemy: human nature. So whenever a situation arises or you prepare your team for a mission, remember these three keywords: Communication. Leadership. Experience.

(TEAM) COMMUNICATION

We have discussed the ins and outs of understanding the human emotions, and how they affect our communications and interpersonal relations. Before starting anything with your team, take the time to ensure that each member feels comfortable with themselves and each other working together.

> "The single biggest problem in communication is the illusion that it has taken place."— George Bernard Shaw [2]

Misplaced preconceptions have to be taken down, and proper understanding of every one's emotional state and communication styles have to be established. Once created, clear communication channels and interpersonal trust will actively reduce the risk of errors or problems arising with every word shared. Efficiency will in turn increase as the need for verbal communication reduces and the team starts to know and understand each other better. With a solid foundation for trust set up, you are now able to carry on.

(TEAM) LEADERSHIP

It is only once mutual trust has been established that a leader can then share their vision unhindered by miscommunications or prejudice. It will fall on you to ensure that they work together as a cohesive unit:

Understanding each member's strengths and weaknesses, ensuring that they have received the training required to equip them for the task at hand, and guiding them towards the performance and safety targets.

"Leadership is an action, not a position." – Donald McGannon [3]

You will often have to change roles between Leader and Manager, but always be there for your team as they struggle (they will struggle) and as they achieve success. Lead by example, and be the first to demonstrate the communication and skills you require from your team. Enable them to achieve the goal through their own abilities and strengths, and Inspire them to unite and work as one, and not individual self-declared superheroes.

(TEAM) EXPERIENCE

Is *experience* the ultimate path to *knowledge*? A soldier may train, but only battle will reveal his true inner strength. In our highly sophisticated and evolved domains, we all train to achieve some ultimate performance goals. Yet we have all faced the age old conundrum once the training was over: No one would hire us due to the lack of experience. But without a job, how would we gain that oh-so-important experience?

Why is experience so highly valued and regarded?

> *"People grow through experience if they meet life honestly and courageously. This is how character is built." – Eleanor Roosevelt*

Experience is what molds us into professionals. A degree or a certificate can prove you have acquired skills and knowledge, but experience is what will one day define your success in the face of adversity. With every day, every flight, every achievement or failure, embrace the story, the lessons, the experience that you have acquired through it.

As a leader or a team member, your experience will allow you to perceive beyond mere facts and give you a broader vision. This new perspective is what you need to carry on and stop problems in their tracks before they happen or threaten your operation. That new perspective will also give you the edge you need to move your team forward ahead of the game, and achieve greater success than you could even anticipate.

Once skills and knowledge are no longer a factor, an experienced team can now focus on innovating, using their creativity and newly acquired freedom to then propel themselves outside of the age-old "box", find new ways to achieve goals and enhance the operation as a whole.

With experience, you have molded your team from Super-Egos to Super-Heroes. With experience, you have moved your operational ground-zero from "capable" to "expert", from "reactionary" to "visionary", from "target oriented" to "opportunity driven".

THE END, OR THE BEGINNING?

By now you are probably wondering how, after all is said and done, my original story ends. How did I juggle my pilot duties, my personal skill comfort level, and the concerns of my crew regarding a less-than-appealing weather forecast.

Did we go? Dare I challenge Mother Nature? Or did I put my crews' concerns ahead of the mission's needs? I can't tell you. Or rather, I will not tell you. I've given you the tools and knowledge, and now it is your turn to write your own stories and (safe) endings.

While our journey together ends here, your team's success is only dawning. With these "powers" in hand, the potential is endless.

Much has been said, and so much more remains. Yet a few words will now suffice: Communication. Leadership. Experience.

Any self-respecting group of superheroes like to name themselves. The Avengers, The Justice League... James T. Kirk! I offer you THE T.E.A.M. – Some of them are very intelligent. Some of them are very bold. Most of them are very skilled. All of them are flawed. And they need a leader. Are you ready?

Experience is living through what killed others. – Dr. Huntzinger

GLOSSARY

A

A330 Airbus A-330

AFM Airplane Flight Manual

ATC Air Traffic Control

C

CFIT Controlled Flight Into Terrain

CISD Critical Incident Stress Debriefing

COM Company Operations Manual

CRM Crew Resource Management

E

EiQ Emotional Intelligence Quotient

F

FAA Federal Aviation Agency

FMS Flight Management System

FO First Officer

G

GPS Global Positioning System

I

ICAO International Civil Aviation Organization

IFR Instrument Flight Rules

ILS Instrument Landing System

IMC Instrument Meteorological Conditions

M

MEDEVAC Medical Evacuation

N

NTSB National Transportation Safety Board

O

OODA Loop Observe Orient Decide Act decision making system

P

PC12 Pilatus PC12, a single-engine turbine powered aircraft.

PF Pilot Flying

PIC Pilot In Command

PM Pilot Monitoring

POH Pilot Operating Handbook

S

SA Situational Awareness

SHELL Model Software; Hardware; Environment; Liveware (Liveware) Human Factors model

SOP Standard Operating Procedures

T

T.E.A.M. Threat & Error Assessment & Management

V

VFR Visual Flight Rules

VMC Visual Meteorological Conditions

VOR VHF Omni Directional Radio Range

REFERENCE WORKS & BIBLIOGRAPHY

TEAM Definition

1. Federal Aviation Administration. (2004). *Crew resource management training (FAA Publication No. AC-120-51E)*. Washington, DC: U.S. Department of Transportation.

2. NTSB report: Eastern Airlines, Inc, L–1011, N310EA, Miami, Florida, December 29, 1972, NTSB (report number AAR–73/14), June 14, 1973

3. APA, *Making Air Travel Safer Through Crew Resource Management* (CRM), (2004)2. Cacciabue, P.C. (2004). *Guide to applying human factors methods: Human error and accident management in safety critical systems.* London: Springer–Verlag London Ltd, 2004.

4. Hawkins, F.H., & Orlady, H.W. (Ed.). (1993). *Human factors in flight* (2nd ed.). England: Avebury Technical, 1993.

5. Campbell, R.D., & Bagshaw, M. (2002). *Human performance and limitations in aviation* (3rded.). United Kingdom: Blackwell Science Ltd, 2002.

6. International Civil Aviation Organisation (1993). *Human factors digest no 7: Investigation of human factors in accidents and incidents.* Montreal: ICAO, 1993.

7. Johnston, N., McDonald, N., & Fuller, R. (Eds). (2001). *Aviation psychology in practice.* England: Ashgate Publishing Ltd, 2001.

8. Keightley, A. (2004). *190.216 human factors study guide.* Palmerston North: Massey University, 2004.

9. Maurino, D. (2005). *Threat and error management (TEM).* Retrieved August 17, 2009 from the World Wide Web: http://www.flightsafety.org/doc/tem/maurino.doc

10. Wiegmann, D.A., & Shappell, S.A. (2003). *A human error approach to aviation accident analysis: The human factors analysis and classification system.* England: Ashgate Publishing Ltd, 2003.

11. CAP 719 -Fundamental Human Factors Concepts *(previously ICAO Digest No. 1)* http://www.caa.co.uk/docs/33/CAP719.PDF

12. Skybrary, ICAO SHELL Model (http://www.skybrary.aero/index.php/ICAO_SHELL_Model)

13. Capt. Al Haynes (May 24, 1991). *United Airlines Inc. McDonnel Douglas DC-8-61, N8082U Portland, Oregon: December 28, 1978.* National Transportation Safety Board. 1978. 9 (15/64). Retrieved from www.libraryonline.erau.edu

14. Atlas Aviation: The SHELL model: http://www.atlasaviation.com/AviationLibrary/FundamentalHumanFactors Concepts/FundamentalHumanFactorsConcepts5.htm

15. "Aircraft Accident Report AVIANCA, The Airline of Colombia Boeing 707-321 B, HK 2016 - Fuel Exhaustion Cove Neck, New York". National Transportation Safety Board. January 25, 1990

16. First Air Flight 6560, Boeing 737 Accident, 20 August 2011, Resolute Bay . Transportation Safety Board of Canada Aviation Investigation Report A11H0002

17. National Transportation Safety Board, Aircraft Accident Report 90-06 http://www.airdisaster.com/reports/ntsb/AAR90-06.pdf

18. Robert L. Helmreich, James R. Klinect, & John A. Wilhelm. (1998). *Models of Threat, Error and CRM in Flight Operations.* Austin, Texas: University of Texas at Austin, Dept. of Psychology

19. Skybrary, Threat and Error Management (TEM) in flight operations. Retrieved from the internet January 2015. http://www.skybrary.aero/index.php/ICAO_SHELL_Model

Additional Reading:

Edkins, G., & Pfister, P. (Eds.). (2003). *Innovation and consolidation in aviation: Selected contributions to the Australian aviation psychology symposium 2000.* England: Ashgate Publishing Ltd, 2003.

Wiener, E.L., & Nagel, D.C. (Eds). (1988). *Human factors in aviation.* California: Academic Press Inc, 1988.

Civil Aviation Authority: Safety Regulation Group – Fundamental Human Factors Concepts http://www.caa.co.uk/docs/33/CAP719.PDF

FAA Advisory Circular: Crew Resource Management Training: http://www.faa.gov/documentLibrary/media/Advisory_Circular/AC120-51e.pdf

Aviation Knowledge: http://aviationknowledge.wikidot.com/aviation:shell-model

TEAM Assessment

1. Freedman et al. *Handle With Care: Emotional Intelligence Activity Book*

2. Byron Stock & Associates, *Emotional Intelligence.* Retrieved from the internet April 27th 2014: www.byronstock.com

3. Goleman, D. (1998). *Working with emotional intelligence.* New York: Bantam Books, 1998

4. Goleman D. (1998). *What Makes A Leader.* US: Best of Harvard Business Review, 1998

5. Covey, Stephen R (2015). *The 7 habits of Highly Effective People.* Miami: Mango Media Inc.

6. Boser R.J. (2005). *Rushing to Die.* Retrieved from http://airlinesafety.com/editorials/Singapore006.htm April 27, 2014

7. *ASN Aircraft accident Boeing 747-412 9V-SPK Taipei-Chiang Kai Shek Airport (TPE).* Aviation-safety.net. Retrieved 2008-10-31.

8. Ciavarelly A. P., Ed.D. (2001). *Flight Safety Digest: Human Factors Checlist Provides Tool for Accident/Incident Investigation.* US: Flight Safety Foundation, 2001.

TEAM Communication:

1. Ladkin P.B. (2004). *Air Transat Flight 236: The Azores Glider*. Germany: RVS Group, University of Bielefeld, 2004. Retrieved from http://www.rvs.uni-bielefeld.de   April   2014

2. Anthony P. Ciavarelli, Ed.D. (2001). *Flight Safety Digest: Human Factors Checlist Provides Tool for Accident/Incident Investigation*. US: Flight Safety Foundation, 2001.

3. Sharren J. *The Birds*. Retrieved from www.ethos.ca, April 2014

Additional Reading:

4   Communications   Styles (http://www.maximumadvantage.com/four-styles-of-communication.html)
Effective Communication With Different Personality Types | eHow.com (http://www.ehow.com/way_5587639_effective-communication-different-personality-types.html#ixzz2FoWkEoUH)
Communicating   your   story (http://www.entrequest.com/communicating-your-story-to-the-four-personality-types/)

TEAM Work

1. *Interim report on the accident on 1 June 2009 to the Airbus A330-203 registered F-GZCP operated by Air France flight AF 447 Rio de Janeiro*. Paris: Bureau d'Enquêtes et d'Analyses pour la sécurité de l'aviation civile (BEA), 2009. Retrieved from www.bea.aero   July   2009.

2. *Accident Report NTSB/AAR-10/01 PB2010-910401*. Washington DC: National Transportation Safety Board, Adopted February 2, 2010

3. *Aircraft Accident Report NTSB/AAR-10/03, PB2010-910403*. Washington DC: National Transportation Safety Board, Adopted May 4, 2010

4. *US Airways Flight 1549 Crew receive prestigious Guild of Air Pilots and Air Navigators Award*. London: Guild of Air Pilots and Air Navigators. January 22, 2009.

Retrieved   August   2009.

5. MSN.com (2011). *60 Minutes: Captain Fantastic.* Retrieved from Au.MSN.com, April   2014

6. Zay, L. (2011). *Hero Quantas Pilot Says A380 'completely safe'.* Retrieved from AOL.com,   April   2014

7. Sandilands, B. (2011). *QF32 Captain responds to discussion on pilot experience.* Retrieved   from   Crikey.com.au,   April   1014

8. Sorensen C. (2011), *Cockpit Crisis.* Toronto: Maclean's Magazine, 2011. Retrieved from www.Macleans.ca April 2014

TEAM Awareness

1. *Aircraft Accident Report AAR-73/14.* Washington DC: National Transportation Safety   Board,   June   14,   1973,   retrieved   October   9,   2012

2. *Accident Report NTSB/AAR-10/01 PB2010-910401.* Washington DC: National Transportation   Safety   Board,   Adopted   February   2,   2010

3. Hartel, Smith, & Prince, 1991; Merket, Bergondy, & Cuevas-Mesa, 1997; Nullmeyer,   Stella,   Montijo,   &   Harden,   2005

4. Ciavarelly A. P., Ed.D. (2001). *Flight Safety Digest: Human Factors Checlist Provides Tool for Accident/Incident Investigation.* US: Flight Safety Foundation, 2001.

5. *Aircraft Accident Report AAR-79/7.* Washington DC: National Transportation Safety Board, December 28, 1978, Retrieved from http://libraryonline.erau.edu August 2014

6. Endsley, M. R. (1995). *Toward a theory of situation awareness in dynamic systems.* Mahwah,   NJ: LEA,   1995

7. Mica Endsley, Ph.D., President, SA Technologies. Adapted from Endsley, M. R. & Jones, W. M. (1997). *Situation awareness, information dominance, and information warfare (No. AL/CF-TR-1997-0156).* Wright-Patterson AFB, OH:

United   States   Air   Force   Armstrong   Laboratory.

8. Chappell S.L., *Managing situation awareness on the flight deck - or the next best thing to a crystal ball*. NASA Aviation Safety Reporting System. Retrieved from http://www.crm-devel.org   July   2014

9. Boyd J.R. (1996) *The Essence of Winning and Losing*. Atlanta: Defense and the National Interest, 2012. Retrieved from www.dnipogo.org April 2014

10. Sapp B.(2012). *Is your decision tempo fast enough?* Economy Heroes, Retrieved from youdontscare.wordpress.com, April 2014

TEAM Management

1. Marino, S.F. *The Difference Between Managing and Leading.* Industry Week, June 17, 1999

2. Townsend P., Gebhardt J. (1999), *Five Star Leadership: The Art and Strategy of Creating Leaders at Every Level*, Hoboken, NJ: Wiley, 1999
3. Khilawala R. (2013), *List of different types of management styles.* Retrived from Buzzle.com April 2014
4. Caan, J. (2013), *My insight: Are you a Leader, or a Manager?* Retrieved from www.LinkedIn.com May 2014
5. Marquet, L.David, *Turn the Ship Around!: A True Story of Turning Followers into Leaders*, Portfolio, 2013
6. Murray, A. (2010), *The Wall Street Journal Essential Guide to Management*. New York: Harper Collins Publishers, 2010

Additional Reading:
Sanborn, M. (2012) *9 differences between managers and leaders.* www.MarkSanborn.com

Chartered Management Institute, *The importance of Effective Management.* www.Businesscasestudies.co.uk

The Wall Street Journal, *Leadership Styles.* http://guides.wsj.com

Linssen, M. (2012) *Why Management Rocks, and Leadership sucks.* www.martijnlinssen.com

TEAM Cohesion

1. Ciavarelly A. P., Ed.D. (2001). *Flight Safety Digest: Human Factors Checlist Provides Tool for Accident/Incident Investigation*. US: Flight Safety Foundation, 2001.

2. Lazarus, R.S. (1966). Psychological Stress and the Coping Process. New York: McGraw-Hill.)

3. Federal Aviation Agency (2013). Chapter 17: Aeronautical Decision-Making. *Pilot's Handbook of Aeronautical Knowledge*. Washington DC: FAA.

TEAM Review

1. Shalev, A. M.D. (1991) *Historical Group Debriefing Following Combat.* Fort Detrick, Maryland: U.S. Army Medical Research and Development Command.

2. *SLA Marshall's Contribution to CISD.* Retrieved from www.BizHosting.com

3. Dyregrov, A. (1997). The Process in Psychological Debriefings. *Journal of Traumatic Stress 10(4).*

4. Parkinson, F. (1997). Critical incident debriefing : understanding and dealing with trauma. London, UK: Souvenir Press.

5. Lederman, L. (1992). Debriefing: toward a systematic assessment of theory and practice. *Simulation & Gaming*, Vol. 23, No. 2., pp. 145-160 Key: citeulike:759978

6. Kinchin, D. (2007). A Guide to Psychological Debriefing: Managing Emotional Decompression and Post-Traumatic Stress Disorder. Philadelphia: Jessica Kingsley Publishers.

Additional Reading:

Maria Overstreet, PhD, RN, CCNS. *The Art and Science of Debriefing*

TEAM Success

1. Tenerife Information Centre. *The Tenerife Airport Disaster - the worst in aviation history.* Retrieved from www.tenerife-information-centre.com , May 2014

2. Shaw, G.B., & Caroselli, M. (2000). *Leadership Skills for Managers.* New York: McGraw-Hill

3. Walter, E. (2013). *50 Heavyweight Leadership Quotes.* Retrieved from www.Forbes.com, May 2014

CPSIA information can be obtained
at www.ICGtesting.com
Printed in the USA
LVHW050804210820
663741LV00013B/1349

9 781497 374614